The Well of Sorrow

The Well of Sorrow

A Memoir

Diana English

SHE WRITES PRESS

Published 2025
Printed in the United States of America
Print ISBN: 978-1-64742-876-1
E-ISBN: 978-1-64742-877-8
Library of Congress Control Number: 2024923411

For information, address:
She Writes Press
1569 Solano Ave #546
Berkeley, CA 94707

Interior Design by Kiran Spees

She Writes Press is a division of SparkPoint Studio, LLC.

Names and identifying characteristics have been changed to protect the privacy of certain individuals.

Section 1:
The Beginning

1

"To Ken"

I decide to spring clean as one of my first post-retirement activities. It is time to clear out a lifetime of clutter. Opening a box labeled, "The Past," which had been pushed to the back of the spare room closet, I see a stack of old journals.

This should be interesting.

As I leaf through these forgotten pages, the consistency and progression of a solitary lament catches my attention across time:

"I cannot open this Well of Sorrow, or I will drown in it." (1977)

"If I do open this Well of Sorrow, I will drown in it." (1987)

"Release this Well of Sorrow, and I will be free." (2018)

No! the child in me cries. *Why should I remember when I have tried so hard to forget?*

I remember *to know, to understand, to ken.* "To ken," a Scottish verb, means to know, make known, declare, or acknowledge. This Well of Sorrow is a place I created in childhood and have lived with since, buried in the bone, marrow, sinew, and the very heart of my being. I created the Well as a place for my five-year-old self to hide feelings not safe to express. There was no place for comfort in my world, where emotions were kept hidden, unexpressed, sorrows buried for another time.

It is time to drain these sorrows; I have tended the Well long enough.

When I wrote this story, I knew that in order to ken, I would have to swim through the murky waters and bring buried memories and feelings to the surface. I knew it would be the only way.

The way of freedom is the release of long-suppressed memories. To my surprise, I found happy as well as unhappy memories.

What is there about my childhood experiences that inform who I am, who I was, and who I may become, even now at the end of my life? What can be learned about the things that happened to me? Is there something about my history that might be useful to others so that they might drain their Wells of Sorrow, long before I did? Is there something in this learning that could help others free themselves from the burden of their actions and the actions of those who inhabited their lives . . . from events that still influence who they are, who they might become? For me, it is time to untangle the past to lessen its influence on my emotional and physical health, felt even today.

I couldn't drain the Well of Sorrow until my parents were dead. While they were alive, I still wanted something from them they couldn't give. Their deaths released me from that binding. My father died first, and then my mother ten years later. It took another decade and a half after my mother's death before I had the time to look back on my life to find what I needed; to ken, to know, in order to release these sorrows and feel, if not forgiveness, at least compassion for myself and others.

I understand that I will have to go back to the beginning. I know death is a curious place to drain the Well. But endings can also be beginnings. Death can elevate the past in ways that help us understand the present. Death is a fact in my childhood, a terrifying force, and death is even a saving grace. Before I can go back, I must ken my parents' deaths.

2

Looking for an Ounce of Compassion

My father, Calvin, is the first to die.

On an August day in 1993, I pick up the phone and hear my sister Patsy's voice. As is her way, she gets right to the point. "Dad died. Will you go to the funeral?"

"No, I don't think so." My quick-off-the-mark response is my internal barometer signaling a resounding "no."

My familial bond is with my siblings, not my father.

I am the third of four children, the product of my mother (Geraldine) and father's (Calvin) union.

Not that there aren't emotions involved with my father's death. But there's no sadness, nor the loss one might expect a child to have for her father upon hearing of his death.

My siblings see an opening in my response, with "No, I don't think so," heard as an equivocation.

Their next gambit to persuade me to join them at my father's funeral is an old tactic. "I'll go if you go."

My older sister, Patsy, calls again. "Come on, Diana. We will all be there together. You don't have to view the body if you don't want to."

No, I certainly don't want to view the body.

Out loud, I reply, "I'll think about it."

Then I get a call from my older brother, John. "Diana, I'll go if you go," he says. "We haven't seen each other in a while." His words are a transparent play on the emotion card.

David, my younger brother, calls soon after. "Come on, sis," he says. "We're all going. We can be together again. Maybe something good will come of it."

If my siblings ask, there is little that I will not do for them. We are all close in age—John is four years older, Patsy is three years older, and David is three years younger.

I eventually and reluctantly agree to go, but I will not view the body.

We converge in Nashville, where John lives. I fly from the Northwest; Patsy, from California; David, from Tampa. The four of us drive to Bowling Green, Kentucky, where my father lived. We stay in a local hotel.

"I'm doing this for you," I say, as we drive together to my father's house. "We need to make this short, get it over with, no lollygagging."

I have no plans to extend beyond the basics. My body is already on high alert, vigilant at the idea of being in proximity to my father, even though I was told he is gone.

My father died at age seventy-six, under a tree in the front yard of a post-WWII, run-down, single-story, low-rent house in Bowling Green, Kentucky. As was his habit, he came home from his job at a laundry and sat in the shade of an old sycamore tree to smoke a cigarette. His heart failed, which seems ironic. I had never seen much heart from him as a child. If there is such a thing as reciprocal justice, he should have had some violence in his death.

It was a peaceful passing: one moment to another, my father alive, and then he wasn't. Maybe the suffering came before death. I will never know. It is lucky the cigarette, which dropped onto dry brown grass, didn't cause a fire.

I don't feel bound or connected to my father. The primary feelings I have about him are fear, wariness, and dread. I hadn't seen him in nearly thirty years. The last time I talked to him was sixteen years earlier when I called him on his sixtieth birthday. I was standing in the hotel lobby of the old Harrington Hotel in Washington, DC, calling him from a pay phone. There on business, I called on impulse. It was a brief conversation. After a long silence, I wished him a happy birthday and said goodbye.

My siblings and I drive across town to the house where he lived. The sycamore tree in the front yard is peeling patches of bark like the paint on the house, but it provides shade in the hot summer sun. The lawn is a dead, brown scrub. His lawn chair is no longer under the tree. There is no porch on the house, just a stoop with two steps up into an open living room. The floors are covered in yellowed linoleum; the furnishings are a drab brown and sparse. There are no decorations or mementos. I stand in his yard, in his house. At least I am with my siblings. There's safety in numbers, and I tell myself, *There is nothing to be afraid of now. He is dead.*

Becky, my stepsister, is inside the house when we arrive. She looks the same as she did as a young girl, just bigger, broader. Her smile and her bright eyes are the same, and so is her lilting southern voice. She has a kind heart. I had heard that she did not have an easy time with my father either, but I don't talk to her about it. We talk pleasantries as well as the plan for the funeral. Becky has arranged everything. There will be a ceremony and viewing at the funeral home and a military 21-gun salute at a small family burial ground outside of town. His grave is beside the grave of her mother, Dorothy, my third stepmother, reportedly my father's eighth wife. I had known of five and had firsthand knowledge of four. Dorothy was the last and the longest.

Before we leave for the funeral parlor, Becky takes me aside. "There is a small box among Calvin's possessions. I think you should have it. It's here," she says, pointing to a door off the kitchen.

I walk into the room and see a small brown box sitting on a metal-frame single bed pushed up against the wall. There is a small window on the south wall, muted light streaming across the floor.

The cot is made in typical military fashion, a drab green blanket tucked tightly into the corners, a precision my father learned in the air force. There is nothing else in the room except two pairs of pants and two shirts, lined up and hanging neatly in an open closet. My father was not fancy, but he was always clean and pressed. No pictures, no mementos, not even an alarm clock. It was a sad place.

Becky points to the box. I lift out two items. I ponder these things as I enter my father's austere bedroom, where he spent the last years of his life. On top of the box is a picture of me at age four. I am smiling, my eyes full of laughter, wearing a red-checked dress with a bow in my gossamer-blonde hair. I am disconcerted to see myself as a happy child in a photograph found in a box belonging to a man who contributed to anything but a happy childhood. I had forgotten that I had been happy once, before the descent into chaos, before my mother's abandonment.

The second item is a postcard from my mother to me when I was about the same age. We were living in England at the time, and she was away on one of her frequent trips to Scotland. Turning the postcard over, I see my mother's handwriting. She has written that she loves me and that she will be back soon.

Wow, actual evidence that my mother cared.

What a curious legacy from a man with whom I do not recall ever having a real conversation and a mother who told me when I was ten that she abandoned my siblings and me five years earlier because my father was "too violent."

"So violent," my mother had said, her voice trailing off before continuing, "that I can't live with him."

Even at ten, I knew there was something wrong with what she said.

During the divorce, my mother offered to keep two of us; the other two would go with my father. He refused. His position: all or none. Soon after she sent the postcard, my mother abandoned all of us.

Why would he carry these things around with him through count-less moves over forty years? An intriguing question. Something to be solved another day.

Today I am here for his funeral.

My body tenses as we approach the building where my father's coffin is open for viewing.

Why is it that in our culture, we insist on viewing the dead? I know seeing a dead loved one can be part of the letting-go process, closure, etc., but my father isn't a loved one. Not to me. I don't recall any feelings toward him other than wariness or fear. It is charitable to say he did a poor job of protecting me as a child. But I have things for which I am grateful.

He did provide food and shelter, most of the time. He did let my brother David and me go to England to live with my mother when I was fourteen. He did allow me to emancipate at sixteen. He didn't try to kill me as he did my brothers. He didn't protect me from being molested, but he didn't molest me himself. He didn't break my bones as he did my brother John's. He did keep us together as siblings. Small mercies.

The best outcome I can hope for is compassion, although that is not my dominant emotion. I am anxious; I just want this over. I don't owe Calvin a viewing.

Once in the viewing room, I realize that even if I sit in the back row, I can still see his profile, his steel-gray hair, his nose above the side of the coffin, his hands folded on his chest. When the part comes for people to say a few words, I decline. In the end, I decide to join the others as they file past the coffin. *Maybe there will be an epiphany.*

It isn't far down the aisle, ten rows at most, but the walk seems to take forever. I keep my eyes on the top rim of the coffin lid, placing one foot in front of the other, my body hypervigilant, as I always was in his presence. My mind knows he is dead; my muscle memory does not, as I file up the aisle to the box. At the coffin, gathering my strength, I let my gaze drop from the top of the lid to his face on the coffin pillow.

He looks dead. His skin is sallow, furrowed, still. There is no life in that visage, no presence. A jolt of sadness surprises me. An unexpected emotion.

It is an odd sensation for me to look down on him, not up, having looked up at him all of my childhood. He is no longer the six-foot-three, violent, angry, overpowering, unpredictable man I remember. He is old. Dead. Gone. The only hold he has left is whatever I hold inside, in the Well of Sorrow, that was created the day my mother left.

We file out and follow the hearse to a private graveyard in a valley outside of town. It is a peaceful place. My father would have liked it here, on the flat of a small hill, with an expansive tree overhead to provide shade in summer and the warmth of a layer of leaves in winter. Once the pastor says the funeral words, the honor guard conducts the 21-gun salute, and the casket lowers into the ground. My siblings and I move near the car to discuss what to do in the several hours before our scheduled flights home from Nashville. There is no wake, no friends to mourn. We bid farewell to Becky and then decide to follow John's lead and go to Kentucky Downs. We have a meal at the racetrack, and John bets on the horses.

As we sit together, my siblings and I try to think of something good to say about my father. It is hard, but finally, we settle on three things:

1. He was a hard worker.

2. He insisted that his children were Americans, not Scottish, although we were that too.

3. He provided for us, maybe not in the best way, but we were usually fed, clothed, and sheltered, sometimes thanks to my sister.

I realize there is a fourth, the most important of all—sibling connection. We have my father to thank for it. He insisted we stay together when my mother tried to split us apart. David was right: something good came of it after all.

3

Conflicted Feelings

Once again, it is Patsy who gets the initial death call, this time about our mother's death. "Diana, Les just called to say that Mother died yesterday. He wants to know if we will come to the funeral."

Les is my mother's companion. My mother and Les moved to Ireland together after Stanley, my stepfather, died. Les is Stanley's older brother. Their relationship is platonic.

At seventy-six, my mother died of a ruptured ulcer, bleeding out at night, alone, on a cold cottage floor in Galway, Ireland. Les was in the hospital, recovering from a broken hip.

I am not surprised that she died. I am not even surprised at the manner of her death.

She was in poor health, refusing to follow medical recommendations that she stop drinking and lose weight. She was crippled by arthritis and using alcohol as a painkiller, something she had done for as long as I can remember. Her drink of choice was gin and milk, from morning to night.

"Are you going?" I ask.

"Yes," she replies, which surprises me. My mother had a rocky relationship with my sister, as with each of her children.

"I'll go then," I say without hesitation.

I wouldn't have gone if my siblings weren't going.

It will take significant effort to gather in Ireland. I am traveling from Washington State, Patsy from California, John from Tennessee,

Peter (Mother's brother) from Switzerland, and Jamie, my half brother from my mother's marriage to Stanley, from England.

"What about David?" I ask Patsy.

"I wanted to call you first. I'll call David, John, and Uncle Peter next to see what their plans are."

My mother was not close to her brother, but he is her only other living relative. I don't know if Peter will come. I haven't seen him in at least thirty years.

"I'll call you back," Pat says. "Les said he called Jamie already; he will be there."

"Let me know who is coming, and I'll look for a B and B in the village. We can't stay at the cottage. It's not big enough."

In the night's quiet, after the chaos of planning the trip to Ireland has subsided, I think about my mother.

I had said my piece to her a few years earlier. For me, she struck out as a mother by the time I was sixteen. I was a baseball fan, so "Strike three and you're out" resonated as a good metaphor. She abandoned my siblings and me for the first time when I was five, again when I was ten, and the last time as a teen. I wasn't open to further betrayal.

As I lie in bed, memories float through my thoughts. I think of the summer we saw my mother in Switzerland.

It was the summer of my eleventh year, the summer that Margaret, my second stepmother, drowned. My father allowed us the visit because it was my grandmother who asked, but it was a ruse for my mother to travel from England to see us. We had not seen or heard from her since she abandoned us to my father's care five years earlier.

The trip to Switzerland was a welcome respite from our life with my father, but it was also confusing. My grandmother arranged for us to stay at a Swiss chalet in the mountains near Lausanne. We spent a week swimming, fishing, and hiking. My grandmother could hardly hide her disdain for what she considered ragamuffin American children without manners or class. Ironically, though she was a classic

English snob, with her British superiority shining through, she was déclassé. Out of the ordinary, anyway, for her time and place.

At the end of the trip, my mother escorted us to London, where we would catch a transcontinental flight back to America. My mother and Jamie would return to Southern England, where they lived. We had several hours before our flight back to the United States, so my mother rented a hotel room for us to wait in. She stood at the window, backlit by the afternoon light, silent as we waited. I sat on the bed. From the moment I realized Mother would be joining us on this trip, I had wanted to ask her why she left. I didn't have the courage until now.

I might not see her again. It is my last chance to ask.

"Why, why did you leave us?" I asked in a hesitant voice.

She didn't turn from the window, but I heard a sharp intake of breath, then her soft reply. "He was too violent. I couldn't live with him. I had to leave."

Too violent? I gasped. *Did she just say that?* Even at ten, I knew there was something very wrong with her reply. I said nothing in response. What was there to say?

But these many years later, my mother now dead, I had a reply: My father was too violent for her to live with, but she left four defenseless children with him. And, even as she said it, she was sending us back to him again. She could have kept us if she had wanted to. My father would not have had the money to transport us back from England. My brothers, both born in England, were British citizens. Why did she arrange for the four of us to travel to Switzerland only to send us back?

I sigh as I toss from side to side across the bed, awake through the long night hours, thinking of the questions my mother never answered.

In the morning, I make arrangements to fly to Ireland from my home in the Northwest. My sister and I will connect in Chicago so that we can travel the rest of the way together. John, Peter, and Jamie will meet us in Galway. David is not coming since he is unable to take time off work.

On the long flight across the ocean, there is more time to reflect on my mother. Her death means the end of any lingering, childish hope that we might connect on a meaningful level.

The last time I saw her alive was in Ireland. I had traveled to Galway from Dublin, where I was attending a work conference. It was a lovely Irish day with the sun shining and clouds skittering across the sky. The lake glinted on the horizon, and the fields were a lush deep shade of green. We sat on the back patio of the cottage, me with a cup of tea, my mother with a glass of gin. My eyes traveled along the length of the garden she had created. It was exquisite. My mother was a master gardener. Now, she was obese and arthritic, no longer able to bend and do the work of planting and tending her flowers and shrubs. Her alternative was to instruct Billie, the handyman, to do what she couldn't do. The results were spectacular. I wondered at a mother who could excel at nurturing plants in the earth but was unable to nurture and care for her children. *Are the skills not similar?*

As we sat there, my mother drank the umpteenth glass of gin and milk of the day. She looked over at me and said, "I'm sorry . . . sorry for not keeping you with me, sorry for the decisions I made." Her voice vibrated with emotion, tears in her eyes, her cheeks flushed. "I was a poor mother."

I studied her, seeing her puffy red cheeks, her thinning gray hair, her crippled fingers, the weight, the weathered veins reflecting her long relationship with alcohol. I wondered what to say. My more skeptical self wondered if it was the alcohol that had precipitated this confession. I was at a loss why fifty years later, she wanted to apologize. She had abandoned me not once, not twice, but three times. *Do I say it's all right?* I couldn't. It wasn't. I was silent for a while, looking down at the garden.

What does she want from me? Absolution? I gathered myself up for a reply. I knew one was expected. My mother wanted forgiveness. I didn't have it to give. My meaner self might have said, "Better late than never," but when I did finally speak, I was kinder than that. "Mother, the milk is spilled."

I took a deep breath and continued, "My life is not free from mistakes, so how can I judge? I would rather not have experienced the things I experienced, lived the childhood that I lived, but in the end, it made me the person I am. I like who I am."

She was silent, sipping her gin. I continued.

"I'm grateful for the two years I lived with you in Cornwall as a teenager. Those years saved my life. What is done is done and cannot be undone."

It was the best I could do. It wasn't forgiveness, and it wasn't the absolution my mother might have been looking for. It was all I had to give. She had many opportunities in her life to make amends, to absolve her conscience. It was too late. I had moved past the worst of wanting her to love me the way I wanted and needed to be loved. I had found a mother's love elsewhere, and I was grateful for that.

My mother was who she was. I am who I am. I accepted that a long time ago. She gazed out at the garden for a while and then asked if I would get her another glass of gin and milk.

Now she is gone, and there will never be a reconciliation. The lights flicker as the cabin lights go on, and my sister and I prepare to land at Shannon Airport. I am in Ireland again for the final farewell.

My siblings, my uncle, and I arrive in the Galway village the day before the funeral. We check into the B and B I have arranged, down the road from my mother's cottage. We plan to gather at the church where her body is lying in state. The coffin is already at Christ Church, the local Protestant church, where the service will be held. It is a small but lovely late nineteenth-century brick church . . . a peaceful place, quiet with dignity and age.

When we arrive at the church, Jamie, in his usual forthright manner, states, "I want to see the body."

"Wait a minute, whoa!" I cry out. "No way. That's not happening. I don't want an open casket."

My mother has been dead almost a week, her body stored in a questionable morgue in rural Ireland, with likely little or no refrigeration. Regardless of our estrangement, that is not the last memory I want my mother. "You do what you need to do. I am not participating in the opening of the casket."

As I leave the church, I'm not sure what my siblings will do, and I don't ask. The next morning, the coffin lid is firmly in place, and the ceremony proceeds as planned. Mother's final resting place is on the rise of a hill overlooking a beautiful green Irish valley with the lake glistening on the horizon. She will be buried in the local cemetery; my sister already made arrangements. Les will be buried beside her when it is his time.

After the funeral, we go back to the cottage. It is an old Irish cottage. The shed where animals lived in earlier times has been converted into a small bedroom for Les. My mother had a single bed and chest in a narrow room in between the shed and the main living area. A kitchen and bathroom has been added at the back of the structure. In earlier times, the cooking would have been done in the fireplace in the main living area, but that was before electricity.

True of all old buildings in damp climates, it needs work. However, the garden is magnificent, a testament to my mother's ability to nurture the earth.

It feels odd being here with my mother gone. Her spirit lingers. Her things are now the last remnants of a misspent life. Looking around the cottage, I see her chair, and the little table where she put her drinks. *Could you get me a drink, love? Gin and a splash of milk; fill it to the top.* Her words echo in my mind as I look across at her chair, the one she always sat in.

She has carried bits and pieces of her life from England to Ireland as reminders of years gone past: the tall pink-and-black polka-dot cat that used to sit on the hearth at The Dock Hotel, carried from England to the United States and then to Ireland, along with the copper ornaments that used to hang on the pub walls at The Dock Hotel, a reminder of her life with Stanley.

She didn't have much from her early years, her time in the United States, her time in Czechoslovakia. A few photographs showed happy times when she loved to sing. She had pictures of us, her other children. The end of her life was a "far fall" indeed, a fall, far from the proper upper-middle-class life she came from as a member of the Scottish families of Clarks and Munros, with the houses, flats, cars, and trips to England and Europe; her life as the daughter of a mon-eyed heiress and a captain in the British Army, her grandfathers and uncles prominent pillars of the community. Daddy's girl.

Back at the cottage after the funeral, Les asks, "Pat, will you and your sister go through your mother's things and see if you can find the diamond ring she always wore? It was missing from her finger when her body was found."

There is a suspicion it was stolen, perhaps by the woman who dis-covered my mother's body. But I know my mother. She fit the canny Scottish stereotype, hiding things like money and jewelry in hidden crevices and spots she thought would be safe from detection. I don't mind looking in nooks and crannies, but I am not excited about going through her personal effects. The idea of searching her drawers and pockets makes me cringe.

Some papers need to be sorted, and Les asks us to go through them as well. We start there first. Pat takes a stack, and so do I. It is heartbreaking to see my sister come to terms with what she read in the documents. She is learning about my mother's selfishness, how she tried to access money set aside in the Clark family legacy—a family legacy left to us, her children. There are multiple letters to the estate solicitors over the years. My mother claimed she needed additional funds (over and above her own legacy) to care for her children. We all know that is a lie. She didn't care for us at all, at least not Pat and John. David and I spent two years with her when we were teenagers, but we worked for our board. She spent her portion of the inheritance and wanted more, the money that had been set aside for us. My mother lived a life of "never enough."

My sister's disillusionment is palpable. She still holds out a measure of hope that there is something about my mother she can love. I'd never seen my sister cry before. As a mother herself, she could not understand how any mother could abandon her children. It is clear from the letters that despite her impassioned and dishonest pleas, my mother was not allowed to break the trust.

Next, we search for the ring, but I know from history that the ring could be anywhere—in a vase, a sweater pocket, under the mattress, under the cat, in a crevice in the fireplace, a chink in the wall. To search will require going through my mother's things. This is something more personal than we experienced when she was alive . . . looking at remnants of our mother's life, her clothes, personal effects, papers, the relics of an unhappy life. It is uncomfortable and revealing at the same time, the evidence of a life that came to a sad and painful end.

My sister and I move to my mother's bedroom, the place where she slept, the place where she died. It is a narrow space between the main walls of the cottage and the shed. There is enough room for a single bed, a dresser, and a place to hang clothes. We have to sit on the cot, my mother's bed, and put our feet on the floor where she bled out.

At the bottom of the dresser, we find a vibrator; it looks like something from the '30s, the wiring bent and frayed, suggesting that care in use would be needed to avoid electrocution. My sister and I look at each other and burst out laughing. This is the last thing we would have expected. It paints a new dimension of our mother not considered before—a mother who was a woman as well as a mother. Our laughter relieves the tension of the death and funeral.

"What are you laughing at?" Les calls from the front parlor.

We look at each other and simultaneously call out, "Oh, nothing," trying not to laugh again.

It is a funny, personal moment between my sister, my mother, and me. A female moment. One of the few shared memories my sister and I have with our mother, even though she was not here. This shared moment somehow makes her more human, a female with all our needs and wants, not just a mother. It is a moment to offset the sadness of her death and the loss of an unknown, and now never to be discovered, mother. It is a moment that plants the seeds of curiosity, wanting to know about who she was.

What was her life like beyond what I knew from personal experience? Who was she?

These questions would germinate for years before I set upon the path to discovering answers to ken, a journey I would undertake to learn more about my mother and father and perhaps their motivation for doing what they did. Could I find compassion, forgiveness, empathy, and release?

4

Happy Times

My father's unexpected legacy of a photograph and postcard from my mother reminds me that I was once a happy child, before the descent into chaos. Buried beneath the layers of sorrow, immersed in the Well, are memories of happy times with my mother, brothers, and sister. There is a faint memory of Paula, our nanny and housekeeper. There are no early childhood memories of my father at all. It is as though he wasn't there.

The first memory to emerge was precipitated by the photograph of the four-year-old girl. In the picture, I wore a red-checked dress, a dress that I loved. Red was my favorite color.

Seeing the picture of the dress and myself with a smile and twinkle in my eyes reminds me of laughter, excitement, and feelings of happiness I once felt. I had worn the dress under my costume for the children's fair in the village of Crowton in Cheshire, England, where we lived at the time.

As I remember, I see myself dashing around the living room and through the kitchen, a happy four-year-old child.

I was excited because I was to be part of the parade; I got to be with the "big" kids. I felt like I was a big kid. My costume made me happy too. It was red, and there was a big "D" on the front. Even though I didn't read well yet, I knew my name started with "D." Pauline, our nanny/maid, had made a costume out of a Dash soapbox. The box was also red and white, like my favorite red-and-white checked dress, which I wore underneath my box costume. A red-checked bow was clipped in my fine blonde hair to top things off. Pauline made a hole in the box for my head, with the cardboard fitting over and onto my shoulders.

"Stop wriggling," Pauline said. "I won't be able to get the box over your head if you don't stand still."

There were holes in the box for my arms. The bottom of the box slapped against my legs as I walked, which made me laugh. Once I had it on, I ran out onto the driveway to wait for everyone else to get ready to go to the village for the parade. *Hurry up! Where is everybody?*

"Slow down, Diana. The parade is not going anywhere," my mother said from the front door. "Don't be impatient. Johnny and Patsy are getting their costumes on. We will be ready to go in a minute."

"But I want to see everything!" I cried out, as I spun around in hopes of seeing something from the driveway. I wanted to go back and forward and just be still to watch the parade, but I was also marching in the parade. I didn't know what I wanted to do more, there was so much to see.

"Come on, Johnny and Patsy! Let's go!" I cried out again as I impatiently waited on the lawn outside. *What's keeping them so long?*

Finally, everyone was ready, and we set off down the lane to the village. It was a path we walked to school every day, familiar but very far at the moment from the village as I rushed ahead of my mother and siblings. It was a happy, exciting day, the anticipation and actual happenings almost too much to bear. I was the Dash Girl.

Every day was sunny in the memories that I had from this time before the darkness and fear came to live with me. I was a sunny, bright, adventurous, willful little girl with a huge smile and laughter in my eyes. My small world was full of adventure and happiness.

When we arrived at the village square, I saw the other children dressed in their costumes, who lined up for the parade to start. We were on time. The marching band was at the front of the line; the parade was about to start. When the music began, all the children walked and skipped around the square and down the main street. It was a long march. We waved to the villagers who lined the road as we walked by.

I was happy but tired at the end of the day, trudging home, ready for my tea.

"That was lovely, Mummy. Can we do it again soon?"

I would not have been so happy if I had not been loved, and I believed that I was. The legacy of the postcard from my mother in my father's possession confirms it.

The card is addressed to me; the content tells me my mother loved me and that she would be back from Scotland soon. It is the only hard evidence I have about her feelings from that time, but my early memories suggest so as well.

It is also a surprise to remember that we once celebrated birthdays. I particularly remember my sister's seventh birthday.

The sun sparkled on the mullioned windows of the drawing room on the late February day of my sister's seventh birthday party. I was invited to attend. I waited all morning with anticipation for the party to start because I knew we would be playing musical chairs. I was excited and a little scared because I would be playing with the "big" kids.

My sister explained the game to me.

"See the chairs over there? We will all stand in front of the chairs. When the music begins, everyone will walk around the chairs. As soon as you hear the music stop, climb up into a chair. You have to be sitting in the chair to stay in the game."

"OK," I said, "I can do it."

Patsy was good to me like that. She explained the rule two times, so I knew I must pay attention, and I was ready to play. After lunch, I raced into the library to see the party decorations. There they were, streamers and balloons. The dining table was pushed to the side, and eight chairs were lined up back-to-back in the middle of the floor.

I will have to be fast, I thought. *I'll have to be quick.*

The children arrived at the party, everyone laughing and talking. My sister's birthday gifts were piled on the table, along with a birthday cake and punch. After wishing my sister a happy birthday, everyone hung around, waiting for the games to start.

Finally, I heard my mother's voice over the chatter of my sister's friends. "Attention! Attention! Everyone, it is time to play musical chairs. Does everyone know how to play? Raise your hand if you know how to play."

Eight hands, including mine, rose up into the air. We were ready to go.

"OK," my mother said. "Here is the music. Get ready, set, go!"

As the music started, we all walked around the chairs, giggling. The first time around, I was nervous, keeping an eye on the chair in front of me and listening for the music to stop. I moved around the chairs with the others, hoping I would be in front of a chair when the music stopped. In this case, smaller was better. There was a chair right in front of me. I scrambled up and claimed the prize.

"Yeah, I got one!" I shouted out, squirming around in my chair to see who was on a chair and who was not.

"Well done," my mother said, laughing.

I stayed in the game for another round. "Yeah," I yelled out loud. "I did it again!" I could hardly believe it; the other children were older and quicker than I was. Each time a chair was removed, another child was out of the game.

I stayed in the game for three rounds, quite enough excitement for a four-year-old. It was a great party, and a glorious day, and it was not even my birthday. I was happy it was my sister's birthday.

"Happy birthday, Patsy," we all sang.

It wasn't just birthday parties. I was a lucky girl because both my brother and sister let me play games with them even when they played outside in the dark. It was exciting and shivery to be a little bit scared but also a little bit grown-up because I was with the big kids. Being scared was OK because I also felt safe; that was before darkness and fear became part of my life. Here there was nothing to be afraid of. I was happy and loved, connected with my siblings even if I was just a little kid.

On a summer night, I was excited because I got to run around the woods in the dark at the back of our house playing "Shine the Light on Jack," a game of flashlight hide-and-seek. Whoever was "it" carried the torch and used it to search for the others in the dark. Everyone else hid, hoping they were not found. Once the person who was "it" found another person, they shined the light and called out, "You're it," turning over the flashlight and running away to hide while the new person counted to fifteen. I counted out fifteen to myself.

"One, two, three, four, five, six, seven, ten, fifteen!" I yelled as loud as I could. "Ready or not, here I come."

The vicarage grounds where we lived were perfect for such a game because there were trees and shrubs to hide in at the end of the garden. There was also a stone wall around the cemetery next door, a barrier we did not cross. The stone wall formed a backdrop in the dark to define the side boundaries of the yard.

The cemetery was not a place to be frightened of; it was just a place we did not go when there were people in it. Funerals were off-limits to us when we were out playing. And we were not allowed in the cemetery at night. Those were our rules. Since the yard had been fully explored in the daylight, we knew it was a safe place to play, especially good for Shine the Light.

This flood of childhood memories reminds me of why I am so close to my siblings.

In the summer before my mother left us, she took us on a sea-side holiday to the Cornish Riviera, a place called Fowey. Like many Cornish villages, the village of Fowey was an old village first settled around the twelfth century. Fowey sat at the mouth of an estuary, a natural harbor, serene compared to the rougher, more southerly coastline. My mother rented a cottage for a month and took us to the beach, fishing and exploring in the village. We splashed in the cove. One at a time, my brother or sister would go out in the small boat to fish with my mother. She liked to fish. She learned to fish for salmon as a girl in Scotland and wanted to teach us how to catch fish. It was my sister's turn. I was disappointed, however, because my mother said I was too small to go in the boat and I didn't know how to swim.

"You have to stay onshore, Diana. You can go out when you are bigger, but not today," she said. Off my mother and sister went, rowing out into the cove, leaving me to wonder what "bigger" meant.

Johnny, age nine, was charged with taking care of me while Patsy and Mother were out in the boat. He said he would take me over to the other side of the quay and teach me how to crab fish. That sounded exciting.

"OK, let's go," I said, reaching up for his hand as we walked across the quay. On the other side, he showed me the steps down to the water and the cove below. The tide was out near the bottom of the steps, and it was shallow enough for crab fishing.

"You have to be careful on the steps," my brother explained. "They can be slippery. See that green stuff there? Those spots can be really slippery, so you have to watch where you step. Let me know if you want help," he continued.

"I will." I was excited to see a crab in the water, so I was careful and paid attention to where I put each foot as we went down the stairs slowly, one step at a time so I wouldn't slip. *I can do it.*

When we got down two steps above the water, my brother helped me down another level and then took out the fishing line. He showed me how the bait was placed onto the hook. He explained that we used bacon strips to entice the crabs to the hook. Then he showed me how to gently swing the line out over the water and let it drop.

"Do you want to do it?" he asked.

Clapping my hands, I cried out, "Oh yes, yes, I do, please."

He baited the line and handed it to me.

I slowly started to swing the line out. "Is this it?" I asked.

"Yes, good. That's it," he encouraged.

I swung the string again and let it go. I watched it fall down into the water and sink softly into the sand below, stirring up little puffs of sand as it hit bottom. We moved closer to the edge so I could see over the side and into the water. Impatient, I said, "But I don't see any crabs."

"Give it a minute. Be patient," Johnny laughed.

I tried to sit patiently, squirming all the time. It wasn't very long before a crab strolled into view, making its way toward the bacon piece on the end of the hook. I saw it move across the sand in the greenish-blue water. The crab blended more with the sand than the water, but if I squinted my eyes, I saw it move along the edge. It was getting close to the bait.

"There, there! Look, Johnny, there's a crab." I pointed into the water.

"Shhh," my brother said, raising his finger to his lips. "Watch! See, the crab is going to grab the bait." Sure enough, a moment later, the crab walked up and grabbed onto the bacon with both front claws.

"OK," my brother said. "We can haul him up out of the water now. It's important to go slow and steady. I'll show you how to do it."

We worked together, slowly pulling the line, hand over hand. The crab held on when we pulled it out of the water. We gently lowered it onto the step so we could have a good look. The crab was beautiful.

"Look, Johnny. The crab has lots of legs."

"Yes, ten legs, eight more legs than you have. Be careful. Crabs are quick and can use their claws to pinch you."

"Oh." I pulled back.

"He won't hurt you. Just be careful," he explained.

It was exciting to fish the crab out from his hiding place in the sand. And I loved being with my brother. He showed me how to do things and took care of me. I was on a crabbing adventure, and I liked it. After a few minutes, Johnny asked what I thought we should do with the crab.

"Oh," I said. "Put him back in the water. We can catch him tomorrow."

We slowly lowered him back into the water with the bait.

"Can we do it again?" I asked my brother.

"Yes, you did a good job."

I couldn't wait to tell Patsy and Mother about our adventure.

We also had snail races at the cottage to see who had the "fastest" snail. My brother, sister, and I got up in the morning, and after breakfast, we went out onto the cottage terrace to look for our "racer" snails of the day in the garden and flower beds. We lined up the snails on the flagstones outside the cottage. The snail nearest to the garden edge was mine. My brother placed a piece of wood in front of the snails while we waited to start the race.

"Diana, are you ready?" My sister called my attention back to the race.

"Yes." Then together we all said, "Ready, set, go!" The wood was removed, and the race was on. The winner was the person whose snail crossed the finish line first, a path that was several feet down on the flagstones. We were exuberant players who urged our "racers" on, with cries of, "Yeah, go on!" and "That is it!" and "Good job!" . . . encouragement going out to our snails.

I named my snail "Speedy" because "he" was pretty fast and won the first race.

"Come on, Speedy! That is good! Keep going, you'll get there!" I shouted excitedly as the snails made their way down the flagstone— going at a snail's pace.

When the race was over, we put the snails back in the garden. I was sure to put Speedy by the flowerpot so I could find him again in the morning. After the races, we went back into the cottage for lunch. My mother asked each of us about the snail races. When my turn came, she asked me what I thought.

"Did you have fun?"

"Yes, so much fun! We are going to race again tomorrow. I put Speedy by the flowerpot," I explained.

"Very clever of you to put your snail in one spot," my mother said. She often called me a clever girl.

We all won a race or two, so everyone was happy. After lunch, it was time for a rest, then an afternoon adventure. In the evening, we sat outside at dusk and looked up into the sky. The cottage was on a hill, so we had a good view of the sunset. The sky darkened from light blue to purple, with the orange glow of sunset visible between the two points of land between Fowey and Polruan, the village on the other side of the estuary.

After my mother died, I found a picture in my mother's belongings of Johnny, Patsy, and me. It was taken during our Fowey holiday. There must have been a shop with birds and animals, probably a pet shop. In the photograph, I was in the middle between Patsy and John. Each of us had an animal or bird on his or her shoulder. My sister's left shoulder was hunched up, supporting a monkey on her collarbone, a chain connected to the monkey sliding down her arm into her hands. The monkey looked like he was in command on my sister's shoulder.

John had what looked like a duck on his shoulder. He, too, was smiling, his brown hair flopping down into his eyes. He was dressed in proper English attire: tie, vest, buttoned-up jacket, maybe shorts but probably long pants as he was old enough to transition to long pants. A parrot perched on my arm, which I was holding straight out from my side so that the parrot had a stable perch. I, too, was smiling, but not as big as my sister's smile, only because I had a gap in my teeth right in front, and I was self-conscious. My sister and I were both in cardigans, buttoned up to the throat. Patsy's had a small white collar on the neck edge of the sweater to make it pretty, and I had embroidery on the front of mine. I would bet if the photo were in color rather than black-and-white, my sweater would be red or green.

Those last months before my mother left were filled with a cascade of happy memories, fun times, and laughter. We were a happy family; I was a happy child, secure in my world. That last summer was a glorious summer, full of fun and adventure . . . before my world came crashing down.

My mother held onto this picture of Patsy, Johnny, and me for almost seventy years. It must have had significance for her. Did she deliberately imprint these happy memories before she left us? Why did she do it? Why did she leave us?

I doubt I will ever know the real reason she abandoned us but believe there are clues, if examined, that may provide a glimmer of understanding. It is those clues that I now seek, as I remember and endeavor to ken.

Section 2:

The Early Years of Grief and Loss

5

Dolly: 1954–1955

Those last happy memories with my mother happen in August of my fourth year. By the end of September, my mother is gone. By my fifth birthday, in December, my entire world has changed, from a life where I felt loved, happy, and secure, to one void of comfort—a life of security torn asunder. I am set afloat in a chaotic world. The only constants are my siblings and Dolly.

My mother gave me Dolly that summer of my fourth year. Dolly is my friend. We do everything together; we are inseparable. She sleeps with me at night, tucked under my arm in the corner of the bed. She is tucked under my arm during the day too, traveling with me wherever I go.

Dolly has long brown braided hair with a red-checked headband to match her red-checked dress. Her eyes are blue with long lashes, and she has rosy-red cheeks. The red-and-white gingham dress she is wearing is like the one I wore in the children's parade when we lived in England. Red and white are my favorite colors. There are two buttons on the front of her dress, but one has come loose. For shoes, Dolly has little black Mary Janes with white socks. Each sock has a frill around the top edge. I like Dolly's dress and her stockings.

I'm not like Dolly. My eyes are green. My hair is a light-colored brown, pushed off my face behind my ears, my skin pale, not rosy. Lost somewhere are my socks and Mary Jane shoes. I don't smile much either. I don't care; I have Dolly. She is my comfort. I like that Dolly has a dress like the one I used to have in happier times.

Dolly is with me the night my mother leaves. I remember my mother coming into the bedroom I share with Patsy and David. She comes to tuck us in and say goodnight, or maybe it was goodbye—I'm not sure. After she leaves the room, I drift off to sleep, Dolly safely tucked in for the night.

I wake with a start. Turning over, I see my father shaking my sister and calling my name as well.

"Patsy, Diana, come now and talk to your mother. She is packing to leave. Maybe your mother will stay for you," he says, his tone urgent. "Hurry! Tell her not to leave you, to stay—she is packing right now to leave," my father repeats in a panicked voice as he goes next door to wake my brother John. David is still a toddler, too young to do his bidding.

I am confused. My mother often goes on trips and sends me a postcard when she is gone, telling me she loves me and will return soon. Paula, our housekeeper/nanny, takes care of us whether Mother is home or away.

"Why are we waking up?" I ask my sister sleepily.

Not quite awake, I get out of bed, clutching Dolly, and follow Patsy down the hall into my mother's bedroom. Even in mid-September, the floor is cold. I'm shivering in my nightgown, with no robe or slippers. When I look through the door of my mother's room, I can see she is putting clothes into a suitcase. She is looking away. I can hear her crying.

"Are you leaving, Mummy?" I ask in a hushed voice.

Her head turned away, I hear her muffled reply, "Yes, I have to go. I can't stay here. I'm sorry. Please go back to bed."

I'm not sure what to do, so I turn and walk back to my room and get under the covers. I clutch Dolly to my chest and snuggle under the blankets to get warm. I hear my father and mother arguing.

In the morning, my mother is gone.

I don't know when I realized my mother wasn't ever coming back. I assumed she would return.

One night I wake up from a bad dream and crawl into my sister's bed. "Where's Mummy, Patsy? Why isn't she here? When will she be back?"

"I don't know," she whispers. "Go back to sleep."

I don't think anyone tells me. I finally figure out my mother is gone. She isn't coming back. I rarely see my father. I am alone except for Dolly and my brothers and sister. And Paula, our nanny, for a while. Then Paula is gone too. David is a toddler. I am five; Patsy, seven; and Johnny, nine. Our lives are about to change in significant ways. I keep out of sight as much as possible. Dolly is my comfort. I lug her everywhere.

By late December, we are on the move. This time another change in continents, back to America, back to Texas . . . but this time we are moving without my mother. My father has taken up with Mary Bridget, "May" for short, a sixteen-year-old Irish girl who worked for my mother in the dog kennels. May is now our new "stepmother." We are packing to leave for America, leaving behind my mother, our nanny, and our—at least my—happy life in middle England. My father, my siblings, and I fly on military transport from London to New York. My sister says we drove across the country for two days, but I don't remember anything about the trip. We are going to live near the air force base, near San Antonio, where my father has a job. May will arrive later, as she cannot travel on military transport because she and my father are not yet married.

The move from England to rural Texas is a rude awakening. Gone are the green trees and farmlands, replaced by a landscape that is dull gray and brown with faded green thrown in from the leaves of the trees. The horizon looks dusty, even though the sky is bright blue, spreading wide across the horizon. The landscape is drab and colorless. The weather is cold when we first arrive, but soon it will warm up. Texas is a literal and figurative wasteland.

The farm is a desolation inhabited by scary creatures, bad people, scrub brush, and prickly cactus. Texas is about as different as could possibly be from the village parsonage and English countryside with its stone fences and tall green trees. We live out from town, down a long stretch of highway and a long dirt road leading to a ramshackle farmhouse, far from the main road. There is a big oak tree in the back and a shed. It is my fifth year, the year I learn about loss, bullies, and death.

The internal environment I now live in is hostile, and the situation outside is dangerous as well. I have yet to learn to squash my spirit, my true self, my feelings. The happy, gregarious girl of early childhood has not yet learned to hide, to be silent and invisible, like a wraith. That will come soon enough; it is a learning.

In the place we now live, there is a hardware store, a drive-in movie theater, a gas station, a small grocery, and a school. We live in a farmhouse for six months and then move to another scrub farm in the next community. My father keeps us out of school for the spring and summer. If we start earlier than that, he will have to pay for us to attend school. He doesn't have the money to do that—his cash is reserved for bringing first May, then her parents and siblings from Ireland to America.

May is small, much shorter than my mother, slender, with black/brown hair, big eyes, and a smile that doesn't reach her eyes. She cares for my toddler brother David, as well as Patsy, John, and me. There is little time for us. May has a funny accent and uses unfamiliar words. We are fed and clothed, but not much else. By the time of the second Texas move, May is pregnant with our first half brother, Little Calvin (LC). My paternal grandmother Maude comes to stay with us while May is in the hospital delivering LC. After the birth, May returns home, and my grandmother returns to California, where she lives with her husband.

May has persuaded my father to bring her family to Texas. The house holds my father, May, my sister, my two brothers, and me, plus May's mother and father, two sisters, and two brothers. These constitute my new "Irish" family. There is a full house, some people sleeping on cots on the porch.

There are so many new people in the Texas house. I want to know where my mummy is, or Paula. One night I am frightened by strange noises and climb into my sister's cot.

"Patsy, where is Mummy? When will she be back?"

"She's gone, Diana. She is not coming back." My sister sounds definite. "Go to sleep."

I am afraid. All these people are confusing. They are all bigger than me except David. I feel lost among the knees.

I don't understand what my sister is telling me and turn to Dolly in my confusion. I take her out in the backyard, climb up the lower branches of the oak tree, and sing and whisper softly to her. "Where did she go, Dolly? Where is my mummy? Why isn't she coming back?"

I have many questions but no one to answer them. I hum a remembered lullaby to Dolly as I sit hidden in the big oak tree, a song my mother used to sing to me.

"Hush, little baby, please don't cry; Mummy's going to sing you a lullaby."

I don't remember much about May or those years in general. We are fed, clothed, work in the fields, and pick up pop bottles off the side of the highway to make spending money. I have memories of tromping through the fields behind the farm and wading in the creek with my older brother and sister.

But sometimes they went exploring without me. Sometimes we went to school; sometimes we didn't.

My father is a hard worker, but he is uneducated and doesn't have many marketable skills. There are a lot of people to support. He was a cook in the army and finds work as a civilian cook at the air force base near where we live.

It is 1955, the summer of my fifth year. Even in spring, it is hot in the Texas sun, the grackles screeching protests from the trees. It is scorching the day Dolly is taken from me. She goes with me to breakfast; she goes with me everywhere. I wake up late, and in my haste to get downstairs for breakfast, I leave Dolly tucked in bed while I dress and go to the kitchen for something to eat. I plan to get her after breakfast, but I am late and have to hurry to join the others. We are going cotton picking. My father has kept us out of school all spring so we can work. Even though I am small, I am expected to pick cotton with the others. We are going to the cotton fields to hire out as day laborers.

Picking cotton is hard. The cotton boll spines are sharp and prick my skin, drawing blood. My fingers have multiple scratches, and even my arms are covered with thorn pricks as I try to reach the cotton bolls and keep up with the others. I don't want to be left behind.

"Listen up," my father says to no one in particular. "There could be rattlers out here in the cotton. Keep your eyes peeled."

I don't like snakes. The mean Irish boy, one of May's younger brothers, tells me snakes could bite me and make me die. I don't know what dying is, but I know it is not good.

A few weeks earlier, I saw my father burn a snake with a blowtorch at the edge of our yard when he was cleaning out some of the cactus from the back pasture. It scared me to see the snake curling and writhing under the blast of fire, its skin burning and peeling off as it tried to wriggle away from the torch. I had turned away, cringing from the sight. I won't watch it. If that is dying, I don't want it.

It is late morning before I realize Dolly is not with me.

I left Dolly at home. How could I?

I feel safer when Dolly is with me. I worry all day.

The hot afternoon passes, the cotton bags are weighed and counted, and we are on our way back to the house. The drive home seems to take forever. At the house, I jump out of the car and race to the bedroom to find Dolly so I can put her where she belongs . . .

under my arm. The scratches and pricks of cotton picking are for-gotten. I don't care that Dolly is bedraggled, her dress wrinkled and dirty, the braids loosened on her head—she is Dolly, my Dolly. I look like that too, messy and bedraggled. Dolly still has a smile on her lips even if I don't. That is all that matters. *I want my Dolly.*

When I reach the place where I sleep, I run immediately to my bed, expecting to find Dolly under the covers where I left her. I am startled to find that Dolly is not there. Frantic, I search around the bed, pull back the covers, and bend over to look under the bed to see if she has somehow fallen off the cot and is on the floor. I look in the corner, on my sister's bed, the other beds, in the closet. Dolly isn't anywhere in the room.

Where could she be? I wonder.

I look around for my brother and sister to see if they can help me search, or if they know where Dolly is. I look in the living room and kitchen, out in the backyard, in the front yard. Johnny and Patsy were just there, sitting next to me in the car, but I don't see them anywhere. I race through the house, searching everywhere.

They will help me find Dolly. I know they will. Maybe one of them has Dolly—they must have Dolly, I desperately tell myself.

I can't lose Dolly, not Dolly! I'll try the backyard again. Maybe Patsy and Johnny are there.

I am startled by a noise. When I turn around, I see the mean Irish boy behind me. I don't like him. He towers over me and is wiry, a lot stronger than I am. He has reddish-brown hair that curls a little, even though it's cut short. His arms are long and have a far reach. His voice is taunting, and he laughs at me if I am hurt, when he hurts me. I know he is mean, and I try to avoid him whenever I can. I can feel his meanness, see it in his face, hear it in his voice. This isn't the first time he has been mean to me. I'm frightened and desperate to find Dolly.

He leans in close, grabs my arm, and squeezes hard as he whispers in my ear, "Your dumb Dolly is under the oak tree in the back." He says it with a sneer. "Watch out for that big old rattler hiding under the leaves at the base of the tree. He might even be curled up around your dumb doll. There might even be two snakes under there all wrapped around your Dolly." He continues to laugh at me.

You think this is funny. You're mean!

I don't look at him. I don't speak to him. I wrench my arm free. I shiver as I think about Dolly under the tree with a snake wrapped around her.

Not Dolly. I have to save Dolly. I can't lose my Dolly.

I know the tree he is talking about; it is at the back of our yard. It is an enormous oak, big around as well as tall, with long branches that offer shade to all creatures in the hot, Texas sun. I can climb its lower branches. I often go there to sit and sing to Dolly. It is my secret place, away from the others, where I am hidden and safe. Now the mean boy tells me there are snakes under the tree, and Dolly is under there with them.

It is a hot day, so I know today there could be a snake under the tree. I heard one of the grown-ups say that in the afternoon sun, snakes seek shade under a tree, under a porch, or any scrub brush in the yard and beyond. This is snake country. Some snakes who live on our place are good, like garden snakes. Others are bad—copperheads, rattlers, water moccasins. Most likely, rattlers would hide under the tree. Copperheads and water moccasins are by the creek.

I don't like snakes. I don't know the difference between the good ones and bad ones. They are all scary to me.

I step out onto the screened-in porch at the back of the house. My eyes are level with the wooden brace in the middle of the screen door. The door that leads into the backyard is an old door with decorative white curlicue supports in the middle that I can look through and see out into the back. I hook my fingers onto the top piece of wood, feeling the rough splinters, but press hard anyway. If I press my hands into the brace, I can raise myself a little higher and see farther into the yard. I can see the oak tree at the back of the yard, but I can't see Dolly. Dolly could be under the tree.

I have to find Dolly.

I am scared and mad at the same time at the mean Irish boy who snatched my Dolly. I can see that the light is fading, so I know I have to go soon. It is already gloomy outside, and the light fades quickly in Texas. It will be worse in the dark. I'm not sure I'm brave enough to go out by myself at night.

I'm going. I have to! There is no one here to help! I can't find Patsy and Johnny. I can't leave Dolly out in the night. She will be lonely and scared. I need my Dolly!

I slowly open the screen door and hesitate before I start down the porch steps to the ground. At the bottom, I pick up the pace as I start across the yard, eager to find Dolly. I can hear the Irish boy's laughter behind me.

"You're mean!" I say out loud, a shiver racing down my spine. I'm so mad he took my Dolly. Anger propels me into the yard.

As I near the tree, I hesitate before going under the branches. It is even gloomier under the low branches, the leaves blocking the little light that is left. I am afraid of the darkness and shadows under the tree and worried for Dolly. I don't want to go under the tree. But I must.

Stooping down, I try to see if Dolly is there, but it is too dark, the shadows darker, closer to the tree trunk. A slight breeze ruffles the leaves on the tree, making me jump at the unexpected noise. My heart races as I move toward the tree. There is nothing for it. I will have to go under the branches and look.

I can't leave Dolly. I can't leave Dolly. I can't leave Dolly, I repeat to myself, breathing in ragged breaths as I work up the courage to go closer to the piles of leaves under the tree.

What if there is a snake? What will I do? Get a stick.

I saw my father use one to poke a snake in the underbrush a few days ago.

Yes, I'll get a stick. That will help. I can poke and prod in the leaves.

If a snake is there, will rustling up the leaves wake it up? I have to keep far away in case it does. I search around frantically, the light continuing to fade. Finally, I see a long stick near the shed. I run over and pick it up, dragging it along behind me as I run back to the tree. It is long and heavy, but it's all I have to work with. There are several big piles of leaves under the tree. Dolly could be under any one of them. I push the stick out in front of me and stir up the first pile of leaves. They make a soft rustling sound as I move the stick into the mound of leaves.

I shiver as I wonder, *What if that is the sound a snake makes?*

I poke the leaves in the middle and then try to stir them up to see if I can feel Dolly underneath. The stick is heavy, and my arms are beginning to hurt. I try the edges of the pile next, pushing around the leaves, hoping Dolly is there.

No snake. No Dolly either.

I'll have to do another one. I can't quit now.

I turn to the next pile, encouraged but not convinced there won't be a snake in the next pile of leaves. There are lots of leaves. Stooping over again, I slowly walk around the tree, pushing the stick into each pile of leaves, hoping to find Dolly. It is getting harder to see as the light fades. I might miss Dolly in the dark.

As I make my way around the front of the tree, I can hear the Irish boy in the distance, laughing and yelling, "You bloody eejit! You're a bloody fool," he jeers at me.

I ignore him and go on poking the leaves under the tree. He said Dolly is here under the tree, and I have to find her.

Dolly isn't in any of the leaf piles. I poke all of them, trembling as I go, my arms aching under the weight of the stick, heartbroken and mad that I left Dolly alone.

I turn away from the tree and stomp across the yard to stand in front of the Irish boy. "You're mean!" I cry out again. "Why did you tell me Dolly was under the tree and that there were snakes? Where's my Dolly?"

"Maybe I put your ugly old Dolly under that other tree over there," he sneers, pointing to a tree behind the oak tree, past the boundary of the yard, a place I am not supposed to go alone. It is too dark anyway. I have been brave to go under the oak tree, but I am not courageous enough to go out to the end of the yard in the dark.

I want my Dolly.

I left her alone, and the mean boy took her.

I am alone in the night, heartbroken, and so is she.

The next morning, I wake up early and run into the yard to see if I can find Dolly. I go into forbidden territory and another tree farther on. For weeks I look for Dolly but can't find her. She is my friend, my comfort, my Dolly. As the days go by, I am immersed in sorrow. I push my fear, my anger, and my grief away, adding a new layer to an already depthless level of sorrow.

I am strong enough in my childish way to challenge the mean boy bully. I tell him to leave me alone or I will tell my sister and brother. He stops for a day or two, but that doesn't last long. When he doesn't get caught or called on for his behavior, he becomes bolder and starts bullying me again.

6

The Shed

I don't want to, the child in me cries. I don't want to remember, to unpack layers of memories, swim through the ripples of long-submerged childhood traumas.

Why can't these feelings lie buried as they have all these years? I soothe my inner self, looking for a reason not to remember, not to feel the desolation buried deep in the Well. *Why should I remember when I have tried so hard to forget?* Because I want to loosen the hold, drain the Well of Sorrow, let the submerged and hidden feelings out of the depths of the Well, let them rise to the surface and release so I can move on. I want to live the rest of my life free of the burdens of childhood.

I learn quickly that I have to be extra vigilant to escape the Irish boy and his meanness. He is sly and torments me when others are not around. When he doesn't get caught, he becomes bolder, his assaults planned and carefully executed. He is bigger and stronger than I am, and there is no one to protect me. My older brother and sister are in survival mode themselves. David is too young.

The Irish boy took my Dolly from me and hurts me if he finds me alone. He taunts me and laughs if he sees fear in my eyes. I hide in closets when I know he is around. Before I enter, I peek around doorjambs to see if he is in the next room. I am mostly barefoot, so my feet don't make noise on the old wood floor, which creaks in certain places. I walk along the edge, against the wall, to avoid the noisy boards in the middle. The creaking sound will give me away and draw his attention. I don't want to draw his attention. My best strategy is to try to be invisible, keep out of his way. I try to stay near adults or Johnny or Patsy if I can. I hide in the closet. He doesn't try to hurt me when others are around.

If I see him going in one direction, I go another.

Mostly I stay out of his way, but it is harder when there is no school, and the adults are away from the house; I am easy prey. He stole Dolly from me, my comfort in a comfortless world, and laughed at me as I tried to find her under the tree. He taunts me with snakes and calls me "stupid," and "eejit," a "worthless girl." He pushes and shoves me, so I stumble and fall. He knocked me unconscious once. He bullies without consequence.

No one is paying attention.

As I unpack these memories, I must remember. The purpose is to ken, to remember, with the goal of release. I try to challenge him in my childish way, and I am successful some of the time, but not always. It is time to remember the shed.

I avoid the shed; the mean boy told me snakes are hiding in there, and it is dark and scary. One afternoon I don't avoid the shed; I make a mistake. Walking across the yard looking for Patsy, I hear a sound in the direction of the shed.

That might be Patsy or Johnny.

I haven't seen the Irish boy today, so I am alert but not immediately worried about being outside by myself. I walk over toward the shed where the door is open.

"Patsy, are you in there? Johnny, is that you?" I call out as I look into the open doorway.

At first, I don't see anything. It is dark and shadowy in the shed after the light outside. Then I catch a movement, a shadow to my left. As I look closer, I can see that it isn't my sister. It is the mean Irish boy. Before I can turn, he reaches out, laughing, and grabs me. His grip is tight on my arm, and although I try, I cannot break loose.

"There you are, you little twit," he says. "I've been waiting. I knew I would catch you." He whispers in my ear, "I have you now," as he pulls me into the shed.

"Leave me alone! Let me go!" I cry out. I shout at him, to no avail. He pushes me back into the shed and shoves the door closed.

"Shut your gob, or I'll hurt you." I know he will; he already has.

At first, I am surprised at being jerked that way and then afraid as I hear the shed door move across the ground with a grating sound, as the bottom boards scrape across the dirt. The late afternoon sun is streaming through the knots and gaps in the board walls as I stumble farther back into the shed. The dust motes glisten in the early evening light as they float to the floor. On the second shove, I fall onto a burlap bag on the dirt floor among the dust motes. I can feel the scratchy surface of the burlap on my legs and arms as he pushes me over, pulling my arm up behind my back and putting his hand on my neck, shoving my face into the dirt.

"What do you want?" I gasp, struggling for breath, afraid and helpless in the dirt. "Someone will hear you," I say, hoping but not thinking it is true.

Pinning me down in the dirt, the mean boy puts his body on top of me and starts wiggling. "I want to see how you like this," he says as he begins to grind, pushing his body into mine and pushing my body into the burlap. I feel the scratchy material pressed into my face and legs as I am forced down into the dirt.

Now that he has me pinned, he moves his right arm up my shirt, his hands on my bare skin. "Shall I pinch your titties?" he asks, as his hand moves under my shirt.

Tears stream down my face, falling in the dust. I can hardly breathe. I'm suffocating from the dirt in my mouth and nose, and my arm hurts as he presses up against my back. I'm frightened, and my mind starts to go to my faraway place, somewhere safe. I think of Dolly, think of singing to her on the branch in the oak tree.

Suddenly, I hear my sister call my name. "Diana, where are you?" Patsy calls.

"Say nothing," he orders. "Be quiet."

"Diana," Patsy calls again, "it is time to come in. You know you are not allowed out after dark."

He gets up off me and whispers in my ear, "Don't say a word to anyone, or it will be worse next time." Jerking me up, he shoves me toward the door. "I'll be watching, and I will catch you just like I did today," he says in a menacing voice. "I'll hurt your sister too."

I can't seem to move, my body stiff and rigid, frozen in place.

"Hurry up! Brush the dirt off, go out first. I'll come out later," he says, as I struggle up from the floor and stagger toward the door, doing what he says, brushing off the dirt.

I hear his voice again. "Hurry up, you twit. Go out before your sister comes looking for you. Remember, shut your gob. I'll be watching."

I open the shed door and walk out into the yard. "Here, here I am, Patsy!" I call out.

"Come in. It's late and getting dark," my sister scolds.

"Yes, Patsy," I say as I walk across the yard, brushing off my face as I climb the stairs to the porch.

"Go wash up," she says. "You look like you have been playing in the dirt."

"OK," I reply, and move down the hall toward the bathroom.

I know the Irish boy is still outside, so I am safe in the house for the moment. But he told me not to say anything, or he will hurt me again. He said he would hurt my sister.

Now he has learned he can get away with hurting me.

He catches me again on the back porch when everyone is out. "What shall I do to you this time, stupid girl? Shall I make you touch me? Rub against you? Squeeze your tits?" he taunts.

"No, please don't. Please don't touch me." I have gone from being mad to being afraid.

"Oh, I'm going to touch you, all right. You better choose, or I'll do what I want!"

"Please don't," I plead. "Leave me alone. Why are you doing this?"

"Because I can, and you're an eejit."

He shoves me onto the floor of the porch. I feel the rough wood on my knees and legs and splinters in my hand as I try to resist him by pushing up as hard as I can. He is too strong, and I am pinned beneath him. He lies down on top of me, wiggling around and laughing. "Get off me! Leave me alone!" I cry. "I'll tell Patsy." He is getting rougher as he pushes me around and pins me to the floor.

He laughs. "She can't do anything; she's just a girl. And my ma and May won't do anything. They don't care about you, and your da is never here. I can do what I want."

He tells me again that if I say anything, he will hurt Patsy too.

I am helpless. If I tell anyone, Patsy might get hurt. If I don't say something, he won't stop hurting me. I don't know what to do. I am mad and afraid, and my attempts to protect myself are not working. Fate steps in.

7
The Boy Who Died Because of a Lie

At age six, I don't know what death is. There is no one to explain. I remember my father flame-torching the rattlesnake in the cactus outback.

"It's dead; it can't hurt you," my father had said. But the vision of the snake trying to get away, the smell of its skin burning is still with me. Death looks and smells horrible.

The mean Irish boy has a brother. His name is James, and he isn't dangerous. He has never hurt me; he is the safe Irish boy.

I know James is sick, hot with fever and delirious. When I walk by the room where he is lying, I hear him taking great gasps of air as he tries to breathe. He can't swallow and has twitches that make his body jerk and arc up, causing him to utter cries of pain. It is scary to hear him cry out, and the moaning that follows sends chills down my spine. His cries of pain can be heard throughout the house and the night.

Whispered conversations reverberate down the hall.

"He is going to die," I hear May, my stepmother, say to her sister Ruth as they are walking down the hall. "I can't bear it. He is crying out and groaning in pain. He can't breathe." May continues, "Ma is heartbroken."

I don't understand all that is going on, but I can sense the tension. Loud arguments, stony silences, and angry words hum in the air. The atmosphere is like a Texas electrical storm: sizzling, hot, electric. The tension thrums through the house. I know something is very wrong, but I don't know what. The atmosphere in the hallways, kitchen, and living room is tense, explosive, and anxious, but I don't know why. I try to keep silent and invisible. *Keep out of the way* is my go-to strategy.

Later I learn the details. In the pasture feeding our cow, Banana Horns, fourteen-year-old James steps on a rusty nail. After about a week, it is evident James is sick. He has a fever, is sweating, and has muscle twitches. Calvin, my father, takes James to the hospital but tells the doctor that James is my brother, Johnny, so James can get free medical treatment. James is an Irish immigrant who is not eligible for medical care. My father's children are eligible because he is ex-military. The doctor determines that James, under the guise of Johnny, does not need a tetanus shot. The records show that Johnny already had a tetanus shot and is protected. James does not get the medicine that could have prevented his terrible suffering. He is taken to the hospital, but it is too late. It is a costly lie that causes the painful death of a boy.

May, her parents, and her sister sit huddled in the kitchen drinking tea, and talking amongst themselves. When they are away at the hospital—or later, the funeral home—as soon as the adults leave, the house descends into chaos. Children reign, especially the mean Irish boy. At age twelve, he is the oldest at home, and he takes charge. He decides what games we play. Usually, I don't play if the mean Irish boy plays. I am afraid of him, and I am less likely to be bullied or hurt that way. But sometimes I forget, and two days before the funeral, I join in the tag game. Johnny and Patsy are playing this time. The mean Irish boy is more than a foot taller and thirty pounds heavier than I am.

"Move out of the way, you little eejit," he says in an angry voice. "I'm coming through," he announces, shoving me into the doorjamb as he passes.

I hit the door hard and feel a sharp pain as my head hits the wood.

There is a whirling sensation as my world goes black. When my head clears, I find that I am on the floor. As I raise up on my elbows, I look across at my foot and see that my little toe is at an odd angle. It has separated from the other four; it must have happened when I hit the doorjamb. In the haze, I hear someone say my toe has to be pushed back into its socket. As I scream out in pain, the mean Irish boy squeezes my foot and pushes the toe back into place. Then someone else binds my foot, I don't know who. I won't be able to wear shoes until the swelling goes down.

When the adults return from the hospital, the mean Irish boy says that I tripped and hurt my foot. No one questions his account of the "accident."

All the attention in the household focuses on the death of James. There is constant whispering in the halls and kitchen among May and her family. My father is absent, and when at home, he stays outside. Angry stares and words are directed toward him when he is in the house. He is not welcome to plan James's funeral but will pay for it. Great sorrow emanates from the rooms where the family gathers. I keep away, staying mostly on the porch or in my room. No one is paying attention, and no one questions how it happened that I "fell into the doorway." Even though it is difficult to walk, it has been made clear that I will have to attend the funeral. My injury is an annoyance.

I don't know what to expect from a funeral; this is my first one. I am silent during the long ride to the funeral parlor, where the service will be. I look out the car window as we arrive, and I think the building looks like any other building on the street. There is no visible sign that dead people are housed within the pink stucco walls up ahead.

Will he be burned and scarred like the snake? I hobble through the door of the chapel into a small reception area, and a larger room beyond that has two double doors pushed over to the sides where the adults congregate. I glance through the doors. I can see a long red carpet rolled out between two sets of chairs on each side of the aisle. There is a black box at the end of the aisle. The box is lying on a platform with the lid open. I see some white material in the box, but I'm too far away and too small to see much. There is a faint outline of James's pale face and body, but I can't see properly into the box. Amongst the others, I slowly make my way down to the place where we will be sitting. We are seated on two sides of the aisle—the Irish on one side; Patsy, John, David, and I, as well as my father, on the other side.

"You must pay your respects to the dead," May says, before she turns left to sit with her family. My father is ostracized; the Irish blame him for James's death.

I don't know what "paying respects" means, but I follow what Patsy and John do and hobble down the aisle to the coffin. As I approach, my eyes are a little above the level of the edge of the box. I see James lying there, very still and pale. I wonder if he will wake up or if it will hurt when the coffin lowers into the ground. I have heard someone say the box will be covered with dirt.

"Hurry up, you stupid girl," I hear the mean Irish boy whisper behind me. "Move on. You're holding everybody up."

Moving over to the chairs in the second row, I sit through the ceremony and afterward go back with the others to the farmhouse. I am a child amid Irish grief and anger.

After the funeral, the atmosphere at home is gray and dark. There are angry words, dark looks, and doors slamming. It is best to stay out of the way, but I can hear the loud arguments.

Then one day, the house is empty. May's parents and siblings have moved out and gone to New York. May, who is pregnant, remains with my father. The house is silent. I am sad for James, but not sorry that the others have left, especially the mean Irish boy.

Once they are gone, I am not as scared as I used to be. I don't have to hide or be vigilant. The mean Irish boy is gone.

May sees that we eat and are clean, but she does not provide much supervision. She takes care of the basics and spends more time taking care of David because he is a toddler. Patsy, John, and I spend our non-school time scouring the sides of the road for pop bottles that we can trade in at the local store for two cents each. There is an old red wagon we pull along the route as we look for bottles thrown out of car windows by passing motorists. The most highly prized bottles are for A&W Root Beer, followed by Coca-Cola. There is a Coca-Cola plant nearby. We range free in the woods behind the house, traipsing through the scrub brush and cactus, wading in the streams and pools of water behind our farm. We are oblivious to the danger of moccasins and other snakes that inhabit the creeks around where we live. It is *their* place. We are the intruders. Fortunately, there are no snake bites.

One day, my sister and Johnny are adventuring in the scrubland behind the farm. My sister steps on the edge of a can, slicing a deep cut in her foot. She cannot walk and is bleeding heavily. My brother, twelve, wraps her foot in his T-shirt to try to stop the bleeding, and then, although not much bigger than my sister, carries her back to the farmhouse. There are no adults at home, and we have no phone. Leaving my sister on the bed, he runs down the long driveway to the road, trying to find someone to call for help. Luckily, he sees a Texas Highway Patrol car pulled over on the side of the highway. Frantically waving down the officer, he breathlessly explains the situation. The officer puts him in the patrol car and drives to the farm. Fortunately, the officer knows first aid and quickly applies a tourniquet, and then rushes my sister to the hospital. She has lost a lot of blood, and the doctor says she would have died if Johnny had not acted so bravely, and had the officer not been at the right place at the right time. Because she has lost so much blood, my sister is hospitalized for a week while she receives blood transfusions and a tetanus shot and the doctor monitors her health. Johnny gets the credit for saving her life. She could have died. We are blithely unaware that other unseen dangers exist. We live in a dangerous world.

After the death of James, the departure of the Irish, and Patsy's brush with death, life settles into a routine. My father enrolls us in school. At age six, after testing and review, I am assigned to third grade, in part due to my earlier schooling in England. I am happy to be in school. My classmates are, on average, two years older than I am, since I did not complete the first and second grades before going on to third grade—I leapfrog ahead, a blessing and a curse as I grow older.

I am never tardy and never miss a school day—not for any reason. School is a safe place, my safe place. I am not as coordinated as the other children, but I play dodgeball and tetherball enthusiastically, if not expertly. I go on school field trips. I am proud of my report card. Each quarter a report is sent home that parents must sign. Sometimes May signs, and other times my father signs. They never discuss my progress or give praise.

Life takes on a semblance of normalcy. I go to school every day. My report card describes my appearance as clean; I am forty-eight inches tall and weigh fifty-five pounds. My grades are mostly A's and B's except for English language skills. I avoid grammar and punctuation. While my grades are satisfactory, these deficits are harbingers of things to come.

The year I am in third grade, the words "under God" are added to the Pledge of Allegiance. We say the Pledge every morning before the official school day starts. After we pledge our allegiance to God and country, the teacher reads Bible verses before we start our school day. The third-grade school trip is to the Coca-Cola bottling plant on the edge of town. The older classes make field trips to the Alamo, thirty miles away in San Antonio.

Life is so much calmer without the Irish, and I am relieved that the mean Irish boy is gone. We have moved once again, the seventh time, to my reckoning.

Now we live in West San Antonio.

Another year passes.

Then, suddenly, my sister tells me that May is leaving my father again and going to New York to live with her family. Calvin works, so there is no one to look after us.

"What will happen?" I ask Patsy.

"Dad said Grandmother Maude is coming to pick us up in her car. We are going to California to live with her until he can sort things out."

We learn that May's family reported his lie to the military, trying to pass James off as Johnny to obtain free medical services, and my father has been arrested. Whether he is in military jail or hospital, we don't know, but he returns home the following week. Another change: I hope that California is better than Texas.

Once again, my grandmother drives to Texas. This time she picks us up, and we drive to Southern California, where we will be staying with her and her husband, Grimes.

I miss half of the fourth grade. We live the summer with Grandma and Grandpa Grimes. That summer, there are many defining moments. Rather than getting better, as I'd hoped, life gets worse, a further descent into chaos.

When will it stop?

Section 3:
Descent into Chaos

8

Another Defining Moment, 1958–1959

It is a relief that some sense of routine descends on our lives. Even with my sister, brothers, LC, May, and my father, the house seems quiet. Thankfully, there is much less chaos with only seven lives in one small place. I am no longer subject to assault by the mean Irish boy. Mostly May is busy with LC. We are fed and clothed, but there is not a lot of interaction. We go to school, and don't go to school, and move at least twice.

When we move into town, my brothers, sister, and I do silly things that children do, such as crack an egg on the sidewalk to see if it will fry in the Texas heat. We catch fireflies in jars to watch them glowing in the night. I bury my feelings of bewilderment, loss, anger, and betrayal in the Well. Life moves on, and so do we. I am here, and then I am somewhere else. The people in and out of my life change continually. I have no control over the circumstances under which I live and often no forewarning of change. I don't have time for feelings; I focus on day-to-day survival. I am an introverted, hypervigilant child. Sometimes it is less stressful than other times, and I can relax a little. But not too much. Change is predictable; the timing is not.

May is there, and then she isn't. I know there are conflicts between May and Johnny. She is only five years older than he is, and they clash. My sister tells me that my father broke my brother's arms when he was beating him over an argument Johnny had with May. I don't remember; I live mostly in my introverted world.

When May leaves Calvin again and takes LC with her to live with her family in New York, my father calls his mother, Maude, for help. She drives to Texas to pick us up and take us back to California. We are to live temporarily in Southern California with her and her husband, Grimes, my stepgrandfather. By now, I am almost nine years old.

Maude and Grimes live in a small, modest pre-war bungalow. The house, painted a faded, sickly green, sits unobtrusively back from the street. The small yard is surrounded by a chain-link fence with a big oak tree in front. There are old fruit trees, plum and apple, in the back and a small garage/shed. Inside the house are a small sitting room, dining area, kitchen, two bedrooms, an add-on bathroom, and a spare porch room in the back. This back room is where I sleep.

My father, brothers, sister, and I are all living at Maude's. At first, it is fun. Maude teaches me to crochet, shell nuts, and bake pies. In the evenings, Maude lets me brush her long, gray hair before she goes to bed.

"It's close to bedtime, Diana. Would you brush my hair?"

"Yes, please," I reply, reaching over to pick up her brush off the dresser. I move to the back where she is unbraiding her hair.

I have to lean up close when I pull the brush through her hair, and I can feel the warmth of her body. She is old, her skin wrinkled, her face long and narrow, and her hair thin and gray. Her eyes are still sharp, although she wears glasses for close work like crochet. I am fascinated with the way she saves her hair as it falls out so she can make a hairpiece to elevate her hair above her brow. The rest of her hair she braids and winds around the back of her head. She unbinds it at night. This is a hairstyle she has worn since she was a girl.

I love feeling close to her as I brush the long strands. I love the warmth. The feeling of being cared about doesn't last long.

I am out with my father, and we are on the way back to Maude's. Filled with dread, I cringe against the seat of the car as we pull up to the curb. I feel small, defenseless, and alone. I don't want to be here. I open the door on my side of the car, reluctantly following my father into the house. We are in the house only a few minutes when I see Grimes standing by his chair in the living room and hear his voice call out, "Come, Diana. We will go and get ice cream."

I don't want to go, but I don't know how to say *no*.

Grimes and I walk down to the corner and across the street to the ice cream parlor. He buys me a double-chocolate scoop because he knows it is a favorite—I told him so the first time we went out to get ice cream. He holds my hand when we cross the road, as he knows that makes me feel safe. Shorter than my father in height, Grimes is still a lot bigger than I am; I reach to just above his elbow. A portly man, he is rounded in the middle, the paunch emphasized by the overalls he wears, and his left ear is deformed; it didn't grow right when he was a child. Grimes pulls me into his side as we walk along, demonstrating his power over me. He pays attention to me, telling me I am special. I gravitate toward the attention. Because I am a lonely, isolated child, I don't see the objective, the grooming, the end game.

After we return from the ice cream parlor, Grimes calls me into the living room.

"Come, Diana. Tell me about school."

His chair is in the corner, and when I walk near him, he reaches out and pulls me onto his lap. His voice is full of menace as he whispers in my ear, "Be still," while he begins to squirm beneath me.

"Don't move or you will get in trouble. I'll tell Calvin it is your fault, and he will whip you."

I don't view my father as a haven, so his words could be right. There are no knowable rules about when or why Calvin's violence will erupt, or when or where bullies and pedophiles will enter my life. I stay out of Calvin's way whenever possible.

I sit on Grimes's lap, glancing down at the side of the chair, focusing on the intricate stitches of Maude's starched, red-and-white homemade crocheted doily on the table beside us. My eyes follow the loops and curls of the starched doily that I can see out of the corner of my eye. It is my way of distancing myself from what is happening. I think if I take myself to another place in my mind, I won't feel the disgust and helplessness as he holds me captive with his strong arms across my stomach. As he rubs against me, I am trapped, afraid, and betrayed. He is gentle one minute, and then he isn't.

When he finishes, he pushes me off his lap and whispers, "Go and find something to do. I will see you later."

I cringe, as I know this isn't a threat; it is likely. It has happened before. Though for the moment, I am free of Grimes's grasp, he is reminding me of his visits in the night. He steals down the hall in the darkest hour and stands by the bed. A hulking old man shadowed in the dark, the edge of his deformed ear visible in the dim light from the hall. He looms over me for a moment, and then bends over and whispers in my ear, "Be quiet. Don't make any noise or you will be in trouble. No one will help you."

His left hand creeps under the cover, slowly pulling up my nightgown, reaching for me. He uses his other hand to move aside his pajama bottom to reveal and touch himself.

"Look at me," he says.

I slowly turn my head in the dark and go to another place. I fold myself into a small space in the farthest corner of my mind and think of myself sitting in the oak tree with Dolly, softly humming a lullaby. My eyes open, I do not see. Blinded, I still hear and feel. I am helpless, vulnerable, staring into the darkness, transporting to another place until it is over, revolted by the touch of his rough, calloused hands on my body.

I know it is over when I smell the semen. I am sickened by it before I even know what it is. I want to heave and instead swallow the bile, holding my body still. I can't make noise, my voice and actions silenced, rigid, and unmoving. When he rearranges himself, he walks into the bathroom, washes off the semen, and creeps back down the hall to his bed. I lie awake, tears sliding down my cheeks, afraid, assaulted, and alone.

In the morning, it is like nothing has happened. But I know it has happened; it has happened before and will happen again.

Sometimes strength comes from nowhere.

I am going to tell Calvin and Maude what is happening. I work up the courage all day, anxious but determined. *I can do this; I have to do this.*

I wait until they are in the kitchen talking. Grimes is still at work. I edge into the room and stand by the side of the door, bracing my back against the doorjamb. My hands are clenched but hidden in the pockets of my skirt. While I am determined to speak out, I feel small and insignificant, nervous, and scared. I am afraid the words will not come out of my mouth and of what might happen if they do.

I take a deep breath and pluck up my courage. In a low, quiet voice, I look to my grandmother. My voice quivering, I move the words I want to say out of my mouth and into the room.

"Grandpa is coming to the porch at night and touches me."

Everything is silent for a long moment. Then Maude gasps, rising up from the chair, a tall figure, getting taller by the moment. She slowly leans over, her face contorted, her eyes bulging, and shouts, "What! What did you say? He does not!" She takes a gulping breath, her voice menacing, pointing her long, bony finger in my face. "No siree, that *did not* happen. You are lying!" she cries out.

She straightens, tall and rigid, towering above me, her mouth twisted with anger. Her left hand clenches and unclenches at her side. Lifting her right hand, Maude shakes it in my face as I slowly sidestep and back away toward the door. My eyes wide with shock, I am bewildered. I thought she might help if I told her, if she knew. *I was wrong.*

She catches her breath and steps closer to me. Her voice gravelly with anger, she says, "If it did happen, it's your fault. You must have asked for it. You whore, you must have asked for it," she repeats as she stands over me, menace in her hands, face, and body stance.

I dart a quick look at Calvin, but he stands in the middle of the kitchen, his face blank, turned away. He doesn't look at me. He doesn't say a word.

I look back at my grandmother, my thoughts whirling. *She said it isn't true, these things didn't happen to me, and I'm a liar. If it is true, it is my fault. What does* whore *mean?*

I am shocked by her response and know by the tone in her voice whatever is happening is not good. I also know what she says is not true. I know he did what I said he did.

It didn't happen, or it's my fault—which is it? Why is she mad at me?

Finally, quietly, Calvin says, "Go outside, Diana, to the yard. Now!"

Backing out the door, I walk down the hall and leave the house. I decide to stand at the end of the yard by the tree. I don't want to be near the driveway when Grimes comes home from work.

Calvin comes out a few minutes later. "Get in the car," he says.

Not another word is said as we drive around, not going anywhere in particular. Calvin doesn't say anything about what happened. His face is drawn, his lips closed tightly in a grimace. Eventually, he takes me back to Maude's.

"I'll take care of this," he mumbles, as we drive up to the house and park.

I stay outside, and out of Grimes's way when he comes home. When it gets dark, I go inside again, to the porch where I sit for the rest of the evening. I have no alternative. Grimes does not come to my room that night.

Several weeks after the denial episode, Calvin comes home and says that Grimes has been hit by a car on his way home from work. No one knows who was driving the car that killed Grimes.

"Your grandfather is dead," Calvin says.

"Does that mean he isn't coming back?" I ask.

"Yes, he won't be back."

Now it will stop, I think to myself, feeling relief—not grief or sympathy or sadness, just relief. The feelings of shame are buried deep in the Well of Sorrow, along with Maude's betrayal, and my father's too-late attempt to protect. New sorrows pile up upon old sorrows: not the last or the least of the sorrows to come.

Fortunately, I don't have to go to the funeral.

9

Switzerland, 1960

Soon after, May, LC, and Lorraine, my new half sister, move to California to live with my father again. My father lets my brother Johnny leave to live with the high school debate coach. We live for some months in Norwalk. I attend fifth grade for half the year, then we move to Davis in Central California. That summer of 1960, my siblings and I will travel to Switzerland to visit my maternal grandmother, Margaret.

Patsy comes into the backyard looking for me. I am sitting by the fishpond in the middle of a mystery adventure with Nancy Drew and her friends. I like mystery stories, looking for clues, reading people's behavior, and solving a problem. Nancy has friends; they go on adventures. I would like to have a friend like Nancy. There are no friends in my life, but I have my siblings and books. My understanding of the world is shaped by the books I read and the TV shows I watch.

"Diana, Dad just told me we are going to Switzerland for a few weeks to spend time with Grandmother Reid."

"Really! Have you met her? What is she like? When will we be going? Will David and Johnny be going too? Where is Switzerland?" I pepper my sister with questions.

"Yes, all of us are going: you, me, Johnny, and David. Dad will drive us to San Francisco, where Johnny will meet us. We will then fly to London and change planes to fly to Lausanne, where Grandmother lives. Grandmother will pick us up. That's all I know."

"We're going to fly on an airplane?"

"Yes. You've done it before, a couple of times, when we flew to Texas from England."

"I don't remember. This sounds exciting! When do we leave?"

"Soon," my sister says. "I'll let you know when you should start to pack. I'll help you."

Still curious, I ask my sister what Grandmother Reid is like.

"I don't know," she says. "I don't remember her."

Packing won't be hard. I don't have many clothes. I do have a favorite dress that is turquoise with small black diamond shapes down the front and sides. I like the color a lot; it looks nice with white socks and black shoes.

I can wear my dress on the plane. What else do I have?

David, Patsy, and I will share one suitcase. We don't have enough things to require more than one. I am packing a swimsuit, shorts, a top, a dress. I'll be wearing my shoes and socks.

"Pack your sweater," my sister calls out. "It might be cold."

We don't know what the weather will be like, but I have seen a picture of Switzerland with huge mountains and lots of snow. It is a possibility, it could be cold in the mountains.

Johnny, the oldest at age fourteen, who now claims the name John for himself, is in charge. John is close in age to Uncle Peter, who is sixteen, Grandmother's late-in-life child.

The plan goes as expected. The flight to London is long, but I sleep when I'm not reading a new Nancy Drew book. I am shocked when I realize my mother is going to meet us in London and fly with us to Lausanne. The trip has been a ruse between my mother and grandmother to get my father to agree that we can come to Switzerland. Circumstances at home with the death of Grimes and May's leaving and coming back probably has something to do with packing us off for several weeks. It doesn't matter. It is a welcome respite from life at my father's house. I don't have much to say to my mother, but I see and experience a world different from Calvin's, which gives me hope that one day I can be free.

My grandmother has a large apartment above Lake Lausanne, where we stay for a few days. This is where I first taste yogurt. Swiss yogurt is firm, tart, and full of berries. I also discover spaghetti, a discovery that merits my grandmother's disapproval.

"What would you like for dinner, Diana?" my grandmother asks.

"Spaghetti, please." I saw a plate go by when a waiter passed. It looked good.

When the spaghetti arrives, I realize it is a mass of noodles all piled up on each other. Ever the practical child, I chop the noodles up into smaller bites so I can eat them with my fork. This behavior warrants severe looks of disapproval, my grandmother dismayed at my lack of manners. How could I chop up spaghetti when the proper way to eat it is to twirl it around in a spoon with one's fork and then eat the rolled-up noodles whole from the fork? That doesn't make sense to me; it's much easier to chop and eat the noodles with the fork. After that, I eat fish and *pomme frites*, the French equivalent of French fries. I try to stay out of my grandmother's view to avoid her frowns of disapproval and looks of disdain. However, I am grateful for the change of scenery. I can see a world away from the one I live in that is different, better, and something to aspire to.

We spend the rest of the trip in the mountains at a chalet hotel. We hike and fish in the lake. I learn to cast a fishing pole, but I am not going to put a worm on the hook. *Yuck!* We swim in the lake, but the water is snowmelt and freezing, so that doesn't last long.

One memory from this time easily detaches itself, rising to the surface of the Well for retrieval. It is the afternoon my mother tells me why she abandoned us, the reason why she left us with my father.

"He was too violent; I couldn't live with him."

I am horrified at her disclosure. Even at age ten, I know this is terribly wrong.

How could she do it? And she is sending us back again. *Why?*

Patsy, David, and I return to America to live with Calvin. John returns to Southern California. When we get back to America, May is living with us once again; this time we live in a house in Citrus Heights, near Sacramento, California.

Time passes, and May leaves once again. My father is unsuccessful in his suicide attempt, and Patsy takes care of us. My sister becomes our mother once again. Who mothers her?

Surprisingly, life takes on some semblance of normal. We spend time with my cousins who live two streets over and go to school regularly. Aunt Daisy is really my second cousin. We do fun things at Daisy's, like play Clue, Monopoly, and Slip 'N Slide on the front lawn when the weather is hot. I babysit for a young couple who live across the street from us.

Babysitting gives me a license to watch TV—anything I want. I introduce myself to Dracula, Frankenstein, and the Wolfman, standard fare in the nighttime babysitting hours. The trouble is, I scare myself—fascinated and terrified of these creatures of the night. There is something so wrong in the indiscriminate taking of life. Dracula is the most terrifying. He conquers his victim's will; they submit and die or become like him, a living death. The takeaway message: there are frightening creatures out in the world who can hurt me, something that isn't really that different from real life. It just seems scarier and more amplified when viewed on the screen, when tangled up in death.

10

The Best Birthday Ever, 1960

I line up behind the yellow school bus with sixteen other seventh-grade students and four chaperones. I am waiting to pack my gear into the hold, board the bus, and have my name checked off the list by Mrs. Bishop, my teacher. I am eleven. I haven't told anyone it is my birthday.

"Find a seat; we can't leave until everyone is seated," Mrs. Bishop says in a loud, commanding voice.

Climbing onto the bus, I find an empty row and slide over to the window seat. I still can't believe my father gave his permission for me to go on this trip to the mountains.

Thank you, thank you, thank you, I whisper to my sister, Patsy. She is the one who asked my father to sign the permission slip.

We are on a school trip, camping overnight in the Sierras. It is cold, not unexpected for early December. I don't like being cold, but the weather doesn't matter to me; I am off on an adventure. Filled with anticipation, I know this trip will be the best! I can feel it. The bus rolls out of the school parking lot and down the street. I hold onto the window ledge with both hands, looking out of the window to see what I can see as we roll along.

As we leave the city behind and climb into the foothills, Mrs. Dean, one of our chaperones, motions to our left.

"See the stand of blue oak in that field over there? These trees can live in the heat and without much water, a good thing for trees that grow in the Sacramento Valley."

It is early winter, though, not summer, and the oaks appear stark against the muted background colors of yellow, brown, and gold of the fields where they stand. California oaks are massive, beautiful trees with many branches that reach out in wide arcs from the trunk. The trees seem almost skeletal without their leaves. Majestic at any time. As my eyes take in these sights, my heart is filled with joy.

"There," Mrs. Dean says, pointing. "These are burr oaks. You can tell it is a burr oak because the tree has light-gray bark and is often as wide as it is tall."

The lessons continue.

As we climb into the foothills, Mrs. Bishop points out the difference in the trees in the flatlands compared to the foothills.

In a voice for all to hear, she says, "See there on the left? Those trees are Douglas fir. Over there is a stand of California gray pine and white alder."

We look out our windows, trying to see which trees she is pointing to and how to tell the difference. We may have a quiz about the trees when we get back to school.

Sitting there on the bus seat, I feel the vibration of the engine through my feet as we rumble over the highway toward our destination. The quivering from the bus matches the excitement I feel inside my heart and head. It is anticipation that has me so excited—for a trip that happens to be on my birthday.

I can't remember celebrating a birthday, not in my father's household. Ever. I don't recall a birthday cake, a birthday present, or a song of "Happy Birthday." It isn't only me; no one celebrates birthdays in my father's house. I have no expectations and no thought of a birthday celebration. I am going into the mountains. That is enough.

Looking out the window, I think about the past few days leading up to this moment.

When I first heard Mrs. Bishop talk about the field trip, I

immediately rejected the idea of going. My first thoughts were, *No, I don't think I will be allowed to go. It is best not to expect anything. Low expectations are a way of thinking, an approach to survival. If I don't have expectations, I can't be disappointed. It is best to stay out of sight, best to be invisible, best to do whatever someone tells me to do.*

However, when I heard about the trip, I wanted to go; I really wanted to go.

I brought the permission slip home to my sister, our "mother" in the absence of May.

I showed her the permission slip. "Will you ask Dad if I can go?" I asked her as she washed the dishes.

"I'll try," she replied, "but no guarantees. I'll give Dad the permission slip after we finish the dishes."

I knew asking him to sign the permission slip was a risky proposition. We never knew what he would do. It was courageous of my sister to do this for me. I would never ask him.

I couldn't believe it when she came back into the kitchen and held out the slip.

"Really!" I whispered loudly.

"He said you could go; he signed the paper," she said in a whisper, giving me back the signed piece of paper. "We'll figure out what you need for the trip," she added quietly. "We can borrow a sleeping bag from Aunt Daisy and sort out the rest of the stuff."

"Thank you, Patsy, thank you!" I clutched the paper in my hand tightly so it wouldn't disappear.

I couldn't believe it! Patsy performed magic; she pulled a rabbit out of the hat! I was going to the mountains with my classmates. *Yippee.*

Although kind, my sister was strict enough to be a mother.

"Everyone has to help," she would say. "Your chore is to clean the breakfast dishes and sweep the floor before you go to school."

I had to be at school on time—no nonsense, no lollygagging. My sister expected us to be clean and neat and even helped me curl my impossibly fine hair when she had time. My school picture showed a young girl with a gappy smile, fuzzy hair, and a spit curl held in place by a bobby pin.

I hear Mrs. Bishop calling our attention again, so I turn my focus back onto the bus. My silent *thank you* goes winging out of the bus to find my sister.

By midafternoon, we arrive at camp, set up the tents, and have time for a lesson on the trees. There are tall ponderosa pines with large cones sticking out from their branches. I reach down to pick up a cone and find it is prickly and sticky with pine pitch. They look like the kind of cones used to make Christmas decorations, and they give off a fresh, sharp, piney smell. Particularly beautiful is the Manzanita tree. The bark on the outside is rough and scraggly. Still, on the inside, there is a smooth, hard, tan-and-reddish wood, hidden from view, beauty underneath a rough exterior. I find a small piece of Manzanita that feels silky to the touch, with red-and-gold streaks. I put it in my pocket to take home as a reminder of the mountains.

"Time to start dinner," Mrs. Bishop says. "Everyone knows what to do."

We prepare for our evening meal and gather firewood for the fire. We roast hot dogs and have apples and cheese. As the light fades, we sit around a massive roaring fire, singing camp songs and roasting marshmallows over the flame. Firelight flickers on laughing, happy children with smiling faces, camping in the forest. I feel as excited as the children I see across the fire. I am content.

Just then, Mrs. Bishop holds her finger up to her mouth and says, "Shh! Please quiet down! I have an announcement to make." With a little fanfare, she holds up her hands. "Hold on," she laughs. "Wait a minute. I'll be right back."

She goes to her tent and brings out a cupcake with a lit candle flickering in the firelight.

"It's Diana's eleventh birthday today." She motions for every-one to start singing, "Happy Birthday." Suddenly, there is a chorus of children's voices singing to me. I am dumbstruck; someone has remembered and cared enough to bring a cupcake. I can see that the cupcake is chocolate too—a magical night.

Mrs. Bishop couldn't have known that chocolate is my favorite, I think. However, there it is: a chocolate cupcake with chocolate frost-ing, with a single candle for me to blow out.

"Happy Birthday, Diana," she says.

I blow out the candle and slowly eat every crumb of the cupcake, frosting and all. I can feel the smooth milk chocolate taste of frosting slide down the back of my throat, sweet and creamy. I'm not going to tempt fate by making a wish and being disappointed. My dream, the camping trip, has already come true.

The feeling of inclusion, being part of a group, feeling special for a moment—all of this might be happiness. The evening makes the trip into the mountains an exceptional experience. I curl in my sleeping bag thinking about the evening, the light of the fire, the sound of the birthday song, the taste of the cupcake. I go to sleep feeling like someone cares, that I live in a world where children laugh and sing songs, celebrate birthdays, and giggle over s'mores at the edge of a campfire.

The next morning, I wake early to the soft rustle of wind in the trees. I lie in my sleeping bag, listening to the sounds, feeling peace-ful and happy. It is cold, but that is not important. I want to see and feel the forest all around me; I want to listen to the wind in the trees, breathe in the smell of the forest, and feel the cold, sharp air. I slowly and quietly open the tent flap so I won't disturb the other girls still asleep in their bags. I sit at the edge of the tent floor so I can see out through the flap into the clearing in front. Looking up, I see a deer walking across the glade. She is a soft-brown color with a black nose and a black-tipped tail sticking up in the air. She strolls, gliding across the ground, in no particular hurry. She doesn't seem frightened, so near our tents.

Then, perhaps surprised, the deer raises her head unexpectedly, her ears pointed. She sniffs the air, moves her head around, searching for signs of danger, assessing whether to flee. For a moment, she stands in the early morning sunlight, gazing in my direction, light and mist dappling her coat. She is not afraid. She turns and walks off into the forest. It is a magical moment: the best birthday ever!

11
The Year My Sister Brought Christmas, 1960

I don't recall a Christmas until the year my sister brought Christmas to our house. It was the same year I went camping on my birthday.

I know this is the Christmas season. I can hear Christmas songs as the school choir practices for a Christmas concert. During breaks and lunch, I hear the other kids talking about Christmas and what they hope their parents will put under the Christmas tree. I don't join in on these conversations. I have no expectations. It is not that I don't want friends; I do. I am always the new girl, and my house isn't somewhere you take other people. I would never think to invite anyone to my house.

We don't celebrate birthdays or Christmas—at least I don't remember ever celebrating Christmas. There won't be presents under a tree at our house. The last birthday party I remember was my sister's seventh birthday when we lived in England, a birthday party my mother arranged. That was when we were happy—before my mother abandoned us. For the past six years, we have lived in multiple places, from Texas to Northern California, where we live now. Our life is not a celebration.

As I walk home from school, I hum the tunes I heard the choir singing. I see Christmas decorations going up on houses on the street where we live as other families decorate for the season. I look in the windows and see Christmas trees aglow with colored lights, holly, and swags on mantels. Outside are decorations on doors and lights on roof edges. I might have seen those decorations up close if I had friends, but it is hard to make friends when I am always the new girl at school, and several years younger than my classmates. My peers are approaching adolescence; I am still a child.

This year the Christmas colors are exciting because I am wearing my first pair of glasses, and I can see!

Two weeks earlier, the school nurse had sent me home from school with a recommendation that my father have my eyes checked. I had been stumbling at school and couldn't read the chalkboard clearly. My father took me to the eye doctor and bought me a pair of spectacles. I'll never forget the day I put on my first pair of glasses. Upon settling the glasses on my nose and behind my ears, I look around. I focus on the Christmas tree in the corner of the doctor's office. I can't believe how bright and vivid Christmas lights and colors are, especially green! I love the color green, and red too—the red of Christmas. A whole new world is before me; I can see clearly.

It is Christmas Eve. David, age seven, and I are home in a dark and empty house, waiting for Patsy to come home. There are no decorations in our house, no tree, no presents, and no plans for Christmas lunch with the family. Patsy, almost thirteen, cleans five taco trucks after school for five dollars each so she can earn money to buy food when my father forgets. She looks after us, makes sure we are clean and have food to eat, and that we go to school, even though she is hardly older than we are.

Today is different, though.

Patsy comes home from work with a big smile and says to David and me, "Get your coats. We're going out!" She laughs. "I have a surprise!"

"Really? Where are we going?" David and I chime together as we run to get our coats.

"You'll see," is her only response.

It is cold and dark outside, but we don't care. We are going on an adventure. We walk down our street and over two blocks and stop at a Christmas tree lot on the corner.

"This is the surprise," Patsy says. "We are going to have a Christmas tree. It won't be big or fancy; I don't have much money, but we are going to have a tree." She speaks in a determined voice.

David and I look at each other. "Really?" we both cry out.

"Yes," Patsy says, "but we have to find a cheap one."

We gaze around, going deeper and farther into the tree lot. We can see a pile of broken limbs and other debris in the corner. My sister motions us over and begins searching through the stack.

"We can afford this one. It's a bit ragged, but it is the best I can do," she says, pulling out a tree to show us.

The tree is scruffy, with missing branches and broken needles. It is ragged and basically a discard, what we would in the future come to call "a real Charlie Brown tree." It would become a tradition in our household in later years to rescue a Charlie Brown tree at Christmas. Even raggedy old trees can bring happiness. This is our first raggedy tree, but it doesn't matter to us. It is a tree, it is green, the price is right, and although broken, it has a smell of pine, sharp and clean.

Patsy is as excited as we are about the Christmas tree, the thought of decorations, and maybe even a present under the tree.

The tree lot owner, seeing that we have picked the tree from the throwaway pile, gives it to us for free, our Christmas present from his family to ours. We don't have a container to put it in, so he kindly nails the tree to a square board. It only has to last until tomorrow, which it will.

Patsy, David, and I each hold onto part of the tree and carry it home, laughing and singing, "Jingle Bells" as we take our prize back to the house—a motley crew, a joint sibling venture. We carry the tree into the living room and put it in a place of honor in the corner. We don't have lights.

"We'll make decorations," Patsy says. "I'll show you how." She magically produces red and green construction paper, scissors, and glue. "Here's how to cut the paper." She shows David and me as she cuts strips of green and red paper.

Next, she explains, the strips of paper are folded into a circle and glued together. Each piece is fixed inside another to make a Christmas tree chain.

"OK, but cutting the paper straight looks hard," I say with a little hesitation.

"Shall I continue cutting, and you two can glue the strips together?" Patsy asks.

"Yes." David and I laugh happily. "Thank you, Patsy," we say in unison.

"Just be careful with the glue," she warns. "It is sticky."

"OK," we say again in unison.

Patsy cuts the paper, and David and I glue the paper together into a chain, our sticky fingers a given.

"When will it be long enough?" David asks. The chain seems long to us.

"Well, let's put it on the tree and see," I suggest.

We carry the chain over to the tree and hold it up. Even with the scraggly limbs, there isn't enough chain to go around the tree.

"A little more, I think." Patsy laughs, and we go back to work.

We continue, laughing and happy together as we decorate the tree. We even have hot milk before we go to bed. My father comes in from work later in the evening. He goes to his room, not mentioning the tree. He is gone in the morning before we get up.

Patsy calls out, "Merry Christmas! Get up, you two sleepyheads. It is Christmas morning!"

Remembering the tree, David and I rush into the living room to see if it is real, or if we were dreaming. There it is: our very first Christmas tree, a beautiful tree, the construction paper chain looped around the branches. Under the tree are two little presents, wrapped in construction paper. Christmas presents for David and me put there by my sister. Patsy, my sister, my rock. Who brought Christmas for her?

Like my birthday, I remember this Christmas as one of the best ever. I remember this tree each year at Christmastime. I remember the lessons learned about family, the love of my sister, the unity of siblings, and the worth in rescuing Christmas trees that nobody else wants. The spirit of Christmas, the spirit of giving, Christmas is my favorite holiday.

12
The Lion, Summer 1961

Sometime the next summer, my father meets my second step-mother, Margaret, through an ad in a newspaper called, "The Lonely Hearts Club." Supposedly, Calvin and Margaret marry in Mexico—I have no idea; this is something my sister told me. It is unclear if she is divorced from her husband, who is in jail for child molestation. Margaret has four children, so our house is once again full.

It is a Friday in late September of my eleventh year. I have returned home from school, finished my chores, and am reading a book in the bedroom that I share with Patsy.

"Diana, get out here, right now!" Margaret shouts, her voice loud enough to carry down the hall.

"OK, I'll be right there." *What does she want?*

Margaret rarely notices me, let alone calls me to her presence. She and her children have been in our lives for only a few months. I set my book aside, quickly get up off the bed, open the bedroom door, and walk down the hall, past the other two bedrooms and the bathroom to the living area. Walking to the end of the entryway, I stop, not going into the living room. I am cautious like that, having learned that I can't predict what will happen in any given circumstance. Keeping distance is a long-held strategy, and I sense trouble.

Margaret sits in the middle of the brown sectional couch, which is pushed up against the back wall of the living room. Her ample body leans forward, her arms crossed. Her short brown hair is in disarray.

Margaret is not tall, but she is large in girth, of rancher stock, with large beefy arms and a round face that looks mean to me. Jean, her fourteen-year-old daughter, also sits on the couch, looking off into the distance, not looking at me.

Margaret calls out from the couch, "Where is it? Where did you hide the watch?"

"The watch?" I ask. *What is she talking about?*

"The Timex wristwatch you stole from Jean." Margaret makes the accusation as she turns slightly toward Jean. "Tell her."

I shift my gaze to look at Jean, waiting for her to speak. I rarely have anything to do with her; she is just someone else who lives in the house, someone I didn't even know to beware of. Jean is another in a line of stepsiblings and other assorted people who rotate through the places where I live. She is an older girl, nothing more than that. My relationships are with Patsy and David; they are constants in my life. Jean doesn't pay much attention to me; I don't pay much attention to her. Except for today.

"You stole my watch," Jean says. "I heard you in my room."

Jean's room is in the middle of the hall, one she shares with her sister Janice. The bedroom I share with Patsy is at the end of the hall. I haven't been to Jean's room.

"What? No, that's not true; there must be a mistake." I turn from Jean to Margaret. "I don't have the watch. I wasn't in Jean's room."

"Jean says she heard you in her room. Bring it back right now," Margaret says.

They don't believe me. Why would she say that? I stand there waiting for what is next. I haven't done her any harm; I've barely spoken to her. I stand silently.

"Go to your room. Your father will deal with you," Margaret says, her voice low and threatening.

I turn and go back down the hall to the room, the one I share with Patsy. My steps are leaden; my heart is heavy. My sister is out at the state fair, so I can't talk to her or get her help. She is my rock. I don't know where she gets help. David, who just turned seven, is too young to help; we have to look after him.

My father is due home from work soon. My only choice is to wait. I open the bedroom door and then close it behind me, move around the end of the twin bed on the near side of the wall and climb up to sit in the middle. I slide across and lean my back against the wall and wait.

I will know when he is home.

You don't know what will happen. This time it might be different, not so bad. Just breathe and focus on the wall. Being the focus of my father's attention is rarely a good thing. There is no hope that anyone will rescue me.

I stare at the blank wall across from me on the far side of Patsy's bed, which is against the wall on the other side of the room. There is nothing on the wall for distraction. It is bare and white. There is a narrow aisle between two twin beds, a window on the wall above the beds, and a closet with a small dresser at the end of the room. I hear noises in other parts of the house, the other kids coming and going. I am waiting for what is to come, alert to the sound of the garage door grinding open. That sound will signal that my father has returned from work, and whatever happens will happen soon after that.

Even sitting, I can feel my body closing in on itself, worrying about what will happen when my father gets home. I know if I go rigid when he hits me, it will hurt more. I have to calm down, let go of the tension and fear. There is some but not much hope that he will stop and ask me what happened. I know this is wishful thinking. He won't listen. He loses his hearing when he loses his temper. When my father is angry, his reason departs and doesn't return until he lets loose his anger.

Finally, I hear the garage door and then the door into the kitchen open and close. I can hear faint voices in the living room, my father's voice talking to Margaret and then Jean. I can't tell what they are saying. It is only a minute or two before what I have been waiting for happens. I hear him call my name.

"Diana, get in here!" my father yells, his voice loud and angry. The tone sends shivers of fear racing down my spine; a numbing dread seeps into my arms and legs.

This is it . . . what I've been waiting for.

My heart races and my knees are weak as I climb off the bed and walk down the hall to the edge of the living room. My father stands a few feet from the couch—a few feet from where I am in the entryway. His face is clouded with anger, his lips twisted in a tight grimace, and his stance menacing.

"What did you do with Jean's watch?" he asks, moving toward me, stopping a few feet away, towering over me.

"I don't know where the watch is. I didn't take it," I say, hanging my head, resigned, trying not to cringe. I want to look him in the eye, but I am afraid of what I will see. I don't cower, which is probably my downfall, but I do submit. My body tense, I stand and wait.

Try not to go rigid—it will be worse if you do.

I don't say anything more because I can tell by the tone of his voice and his movements that he has already made up his mind. A queer sense of calm descends as I accept the inevitability of what will happen. I know I have to endure. I have survived in the past and will survive again. Still, I feel my muscles tighten in anticipation as I stand there waiting for him to grab me. I will have no control in his iron grip and against the long reach of his six-foot-four height. He can throw me any which way he wants, like a rag doll. It won't be the first time.

He towers over me, menacing in his white pants and shirt, still splattered with the food he cooked at his job. As I stand and wait, I can see from the corner of my eye that he is reaching for his belt buckle.

"Give it back. It will be worse for you if you don't. I won't have liars or thieves in this house."

I know this scenario; I've been here before. Time stops. In slow motion, he walks toward me. I watch my father unbuckle his belt and slowly pull it out of the loops in his pants. Black with a silver buckle, the belt a dark contrast to the white of his work pants. The belt looks longer and longer as it slides out of each loop and into his hand. The leather doubles over. He mostly hits with the leather but not always, especially if he is in a rage. He is on the way to rage now. With a quick glance, I can see it in his face.

"This is your last chance. Give back the watch, or you will get a whipping." His eyes are blank, his face contorted with anger, his mouth a thin slice across his face as he reaches for me.

"I didn't take the watch," I cry again.

I flinch as he grabs my upper arm between the shoulder and elbow, spreading his fingers and tightening his grip like a vice. Now he can jerk me around as much as he wants. I am 80 pounds; he is over 220. That's the thing with my father: once he opens the lid on his store of anger, it must dissipate before he stops. His anger store can be half-empty or full to the brim. Tonight, it is overflowing.

"I don't tolerate liars and thieves in this house," he says.

I see his arm lift the belt above his head and then watch it descend. The first slice of pain is overwhelming as the leather connects with my back. I glance behind him and see Jean still sitting beside her mother on the couch with a smirk on her face. *Why?* I wonder, as the second blow lands. I feel the bite of the leather strap rip across my back. Time is suspended, tied to the force of the leather as it connects with my back and legs and the jerking motion as my father pulls me around with his other arm. It is late summer. I am wearing a sleeve-less top and shorts. I feel my blouse sticking to the blood and sweat. He is explosive.

When he halts for a minute, I feel a ray of hope. *Has he had enough? Not yet*, I realize as he draws in a long breath and jerks me around again for another blow.

Then he abruptly lets go of my arm, and I slip to the floor. I scramble, trying to get up and away, but he reaches out to grab me again. He is not finished. I look over my shoulder and see him towering over me. The rage on his face is clear from his mouth, twisted and grim, his eyes dull and intent. His arm is raised for another strike. It is a long way down before the belt connects with my back, sending me jerking away from the blow but not enough to loosen his grip.

This is bad, very bad. Words pass through my brain as he lets me go again.

I slip a second time, banging my head on the wall and landing on the floor. I lie face down, wincing at a sharp pain in my left shoulder as I lift my hands up behind my neck, using my elbows to cover the sides of my face. I am still waiting for the next strike from the belt. Instead, my father drops the belt and reaches up on the wall and pulls down a framed picture, which he lifts over his head and smashes into my back. Shards of glass and wood explode everywhere, down into my back, along the floor, into the wall next to my face. I'm afraid to close my eyes. I need to be able to see movement to gauge the direction of the next blow, to try to protect myself if I can. I lie where I am, silent, not daring to move, in limbo, not knowing what to expect. My blood smells coppery, and I feel the tingling pain of welts rising on my back, arms, and legs. The shock provides a momentary distraction.

There is a moment of eerie silence. Time, motion, and sound are suspended while I wait for the next move.

"Get in your room," he spits out. "Don't come out until I tell you."

I look up and see him pick up his belt and start to rewind it back into the loops around his pants.

He is done. I have to move, right now. It is best to stay down, get out of sight, and just get to the room.

Raising my head from the floor, the bedroom door looks like a long way away. There is a sharp pain in my left arm, so I try not to move it as I go. I concentrate on reaching ahead with my right arm, sliding one knee in front of the other. I slowly drag and slide across the wood, my knees trying to catch traction on the smooth floor. I can see blood spots on my right arm where small shards of glass have penetrated the skin, and there is a red buckle mark on my left arm. My focus, however, is on getting down the hall and into the bedroom. A closed door will not keep him out if he is still in a rage, but I will feel safer with a door between him and me.

I want to lie down, but I know I can't rest on my back because I can feel something is wrong. I don't know what, how much, or how bad. I just know that it is. When I reach the room, I shut the door behind me. I grab onto the end of the bed with my right arm and shoulder to leverage myself up off the floor and to a standing position. I lean my right shoulder against the wall to steady myself, trying not to get blood on the paint. I am shivering, my teeth chattering, head swimming, and ears ringing. Once I can breathe, I steady myself to reach for an old shirt out of the closet and sling it over my shoulder and around me.

There will be more trouble if I get blood on the blanket, I am thinking as I crawl onto the bed.

I curl up on my side with my knees slightly bent, trying to find a place without pain. I close my eyes and wait for my sister to come home.

"Diana, wake up." I hear Patsy's voice. I open my eyes and see someone standing by the bed, a silhouette, the overhead light as a backdrop.

It must be nighttime. I am confused for a moment before I move and feel the pain in my shoulder, back, and legs. I still myself, and then feel relief as I realize it is my sister beside me.

"He beat me. Jean said I stole her watch. I didn't," I whisper to Patsy. "My back hurts. Please help me."

"Lie still," she says. "I'll be right back."

True to her word, she is back within minutes.

"I'm going to clean this up," Patsy says in a soft voice. "It will hurt, but it has to be done."

She has tweezers to pull out the glass and wood fragments, peroxide, ointment, and Band-Aids. She tells me to lie flat on my stomach, and she lifts the shirt from my back. She works for a while, testing my shoulder, which she says is probably sore from being pulled around.

"OK, I think that will do it. The wounds are not deep, but you'll need to be quiet and stay still for a while. It's Friday. You can rest for the weekend. I'll do your chores." She continues, "Do you need me to stay with you?"

"No, thank you. I'll be OK."

She gets up to go to the other room but turns around before she reaches the door. "Oh! Look!" she says, pointing to her bed on the other side of the room. "Clyde won this for me at the fair. You can have him. He's yours now."

I look across at my sister's bed and see a huge stuffed lion with a golden mane and fluff at the end of his regal tail. The lion has blue eyes, long eyelashes, and what looks like a grin on his face. He is nearly as big as I am.

"Oh, thank you!" I tell Patsy as she transfers the stuffed lion over to my bed.

The lion is a comfort on the bed between me and the door. I support my left arm over his body, and it doesn't hurt as much. I am alive, with no broken bones and no significant injury except to my spirit. *How long will it go on like this?* I don't know; I have no way of knowing. This is my life. I keep Lion next to me as I drift off to sleep again. Another inanimate object that comforts me in a comfortless world.

The next morning, Patsy wakes me and tells me that I can come out now and have something to eat. "Jean found her watch in her sweater pocket."

I leave the lion perched on my bed. I don't want to leave the room, but I know at some point I will have to. Everyone is required to eat at the table. I stay where I am as long as I can.

When I go into the kitchen, no one says anything, no one looks at me except Jean, who smirks at me and doesn't apologize. I wonder again, *Why?*

It is my turn to do the dishes. It is like yesterday never happened.

There is nothing I can do about what happened or will happen, just go on as best I can. There is no hope in running away. We tried that once. Aunt Daisy knows what is happening at our house. She helps Patsy, David, and me "run away" to the local children's center. As a foster/adoptive parent, she is familiar with the center and takes us there to get help. Patsy, David, and I stay at the shelter for two days, then we are sent back home as "belligerent" children. We are not children who require protection; we are assessed as children who are in need of parental discipline. There will be no help from that quarter. It is hopeless to hope for help. Even with Daisy as an anchor in this chaotic world, it is clear life with my father will go on unchanged. The nature of the risks and harms change but don't abate. There is no choice but to endure and make the best of it, holding myself and my thoughts inward. I struggle to survive in an unpredictable and violent world. Kindnesses don't erase the harm but help to mitigate it. School will start soon, and I will be out of the house all day.

I am in seventh grade. In the summer, we move again to Fair Oaks, a suburb of Sacramento. My father has purchased a home in a subdivision, a house big enough for the expanded family. He is gone most of the time working. Margaret has creepy male friends in the house during the day. I spend as much time as I can babysitting or studying in my room at the top of the house.

13

The Drowning, Summer 1962

It is a hot, dry, oppressive Northern California summer day with temperatures in the 90s and likely over 100 degrees by afternoon. I feel the heat even more because my bedroom is in a loft at the top of the house, where hot air gets trapped under the eaves to make it a sultry place in summer, day or night. Poorly ventilated, the attic would not be comfortable even if air were brought in from outside, but it is my safe place. It feels like I am baking slowly in an oven, closed in and stifling. Even when outdoors, I feel closed in, though I live in a place where the sky is open and ever-present. I don't like the heat, and I am out of sorts before the day even begins. Fortunately, this type of weather doesn't last long, a month or two at most, but when hot, it is uncomfortable, and it is scorching the day of the drowning.

I wake up early, sweating, knowing I will have to get up soon, as we are going north to pick peaches. Picking peaches is not something I want to do. It is a way to make money for school clothes; otherwise, I will have to wear handmade Margaret clothes. I'm embarrassed by these sackcloth dresses, which make me stand out as a poor girl who wears awful clothing. I want to be like the other kids, and one way to do that is to make money to buy my own clothes. I am going peach picking. I want to look like the other kids, even if I don't feel like them.

OK, I better get up and get ready for the day.

Putting on shorts and a sleeveless top, I also slip on a pair of sandals. As a first-time peach picker, I do not realize that cool will potentially be offset by stickiness and even worse when peach fuzz clings to the skin.

Breakfast is next and then an hour's drive north to the orchards through Roseville, Lincoln, and Yuba City. Margaret, three of her children, David, and I are going to the peach orchards. We have a large station wagon, enough room for five preteen and teen children to sit in the middle seat and a back seat that serves as a trunk when not full of children, which it is most of the time. There is no air-conditioning. I am in the bench seat in the middle of the car, the window down, unsuccessfully trying to draw breeze into the car as we drive north.

Summer at its worst.

After a long time on the road, we make a left turn into a narrow, rutted lane that leads to a staging area for pickers. We are in the midst of a giant peach tree grove, peaches ripe for the market. We are not the only pickers here. I see several cars already lined up on the side of the dirt road. Getting out of the car, we walk over to the table where pickers are signed in, each assigned a number that is used to tally how many lugs of peaches an individual has picked. We are all given a hopsack bag that fits over our necks and hangs down at our sides.

"Here is how it works," the field manager says. "You each get assigned a row. You climb a ladder up into the tree, pick peaches, put them into your bag, climb down, and transfer the peaches carefully into the box at the base of the tree."

Older workers are assigned to move ladders for the smaller pickers.

"Pick peaches on the lower branches while waiting for a ladder move," the field manager continues.

Ascending, picking, descending, emptying the bag, and climbing up again is the scope of work throughout the day. Once one of the boxes is full, we start on another and another, trying to pick as many peaches as possible. The more boxes filled, the more money earned. As I look around, I see that the orchard is full of women and children picking peaches.

Perhaps I am daydreaming; I am picking peaches, the box at the base of the tree filling up, apparently not fast enough for my step-mother, Margaret. I don't see or hear her approach. I am shocked when I feel the first lash of the peach tree whip against my bare legs: a sharp and lacerating pain racing along my nerves, reaching my brain soon after the limb whip tore through skin and welted again. I hardly have time to process before another lash comes across my legs. Sharp pains reverberate across the nerves and muscles, shooting up to my brain. There is another and another, leaving a series of lash welts up my thighs and down my calves. I don't know how I stay on the ladder, my response to the whipping so visceral and consuming.

Through the pain, I hear Margaret's harsh voice, "Hurry up! You're not working hard enough."

Despite the pain, I feel a rising tide of anger, like bile at the pit of my stomach rising up my throat and into my mouth. I am outraged; I have been working hard, my nearly full box at the base of the tree a testament.

Why is she doing this? And then the words, angry and intense, fly out of my mouth. "I hate you! I wish you were dead."

I mean it, I do. I *do* hate Margaret at this moment and maybe other moments in the past, but I am not thinking about the consequences of a death wish. I do not know I am capable of such a thing. The words reflect what I feel at that moment in time. I am angry, in pain, and in reflection, outraged at the injustice of an unwarranted beating. My wish doesn't give her pause, however. She continues to whip me until my legs are crisscrossed with livid welts up and down my thighs and legs.

"Work harder," Margaret says, and walks back to her own row down the line.

The rest of the afternoon is incident-free, no immediate consequences for my outburst and no one mentions the whipping. It is like it didn't happen. Earnings are tallied, and we all set off for the river to wash off the peach fuzz and cool down before the long drive back to town.

Maybe the river water will ease the pain in my legs. I feel the welts on my legs sticking painfully to the hot car seat.

I am not much of a swimmer, so I will mostly be splashing at the edge of the water. Someone at the orchard told us that the river is shallow and OK for wading and cooling off. We are from the valley; we don't know that snowmelt at this time of year is particularly dangerous for swimmers. The change between hot and cold can cause loss of muscle control—something the locals know, but we don't.

The river is refreshing, icy cold, and relieves the pain in my legs, and the gentle flow of the water on the edge washes off the sticky fuzz from my skin. Everyone is in or near the water. I don't know where Margaret is. Dave, her seventeen-year-old son, and the others are to the right of me on the riverbank or splashing at the edge of the river. Dave and Jean are older than I; Janet and my brother David are younger. It's the hottest part of the day, and we are all enjoying the respite from the heat.

Something catches my attention, and I look up. I see Margaret flailing in the water. I can see her mouth moving, but I cannot hear the words. I can't really see her face either, but somehow her fear registers. Dave and Jean are farther down the bank; neither can swim. David and Janet are down the bank to my right. As I look back over, I see that Dave is trying to pull loose a boat that is chained to a wood piling on the shore. There aren't any other people around. I don't think about it; I start splashing out into the river toward Margaret.

While the river appears shallow, mostly knee-deep, there is a sudden drop-off. Margaret isn't very far away, but I see that she is in deep water and struggling. She isn't making any progress toward the shore, although her arms are flailing.

I dog-paddle out. By the time I am near, she is already in a full-blown panic, her face distorted with fear.

Trying to calm her, I call out, "I'm coming. I'm coming!" As I reach Margaret, she grabs me, scrambling to stay afloat, pulling me into the eddy, taking me down under the water with her. We both resurface, gasping for air, spitting out water, kicking, and trying to get free of the eddy we are in. She is trying to grab my hair, my shoulders, my arms—anything—as she drags me down again.

I can't help her. I will die. She is too strong. I sink down, swallowing water and struggling to breathe, struggling to be free of Margaret's desperate grasp as she tries to hold onto me. Brief relief comes as Margaret and I rise again to the surface of the water.

I know if I stay, I will not come up again. There is a certainty in the "knowing." I can't help, and I will die if I don't leave. Shocked and confused, I struggle to disentangle myself from Margaret so I can escape.

Do I see recognition in her face? Does she know I am trying to leave? Does she know she is going to die? Did she look at me with hate and fear? What I see is a contorted face filled with fear. What I hear are her dying words, "I'll get you for this! I'll get you," as she thrashes and grabs for me while I struggle to pull away from her grasp.

What I know for sure is that I left Margaret to die. I feel this intense, overpowering desire to live. I wrench my arm free and work to move away from Margaret. A new surge of fear propels me a few more strokes forward.

Each time I try to touch bottom, I sink below the surface, swallow water, and plunge upward so my head is above the water. The river is so cold and is supposed to be shallow; I can't understand why I can't touch the bottom.

It seems like forever—swim, sink, thrust up, raise my arms for a few more strokes. I eventually reach the shore and struggle to drag myself up out of the water. My limbs feel rubbery and out of my control. I look up and can see Margaret's body floating face down in the water, slowly circling in the eddy. I glance over and see that

Dave has loosened the boat from its mooring, and the other children are standing on the shore. Death by drowning didn't take long and seemed like forever.

I can only think: *I'm alive.*

I had wished her dead, and now she is. It is my fault; I didn't save her. I see Dave is paddling toward his mother, and I see him grab his mother's body, pull her against the side of the boat, and begin to paddle to shore. Someone has called the police and an ambulance. The body is retrieved, and we return home. I remember nothing of that ride or the days that follow.

No one talks to me about what happened; no one mentions my role in her death. No one asks me how I am feeling, how my legs are. I stay out of sight in the hot, oppressive attic. There is no comfort to be had. My father doesn't ask me what happened, if I'm OK or how I feel. No one says anything about my wish, my failure to save, my selfish desire to live. No one seems to make a connection between my words and her death.

Could I have tried harder? Did I try hard enough? These questions are unanswerable, and Margaret placed a curse of her own—she would "get me," and in a way, she did.

Three days later, I sit on my bed, terrified of the funeral to come and the required walk down the aisle to view the body in the coffin. This isn't the first open-casket funeral I have been to, but this one is different.

How will she get me? Is she truly dead? Will she leap from the coffin as I walk by?

Would she, like Dracula, rise from the dead and come for me in some dark corner, at night, when I least expect it? Would she be a "ghost" that torments me? I am already afraid of the dark; I scared myself by watching horror movies at night when babysitting. This is even worse.

When I am in a crowd, I scan to see if she is there, coming to get me. Anxiety and guilt for wishing her dead and failing to save her riddle my waking and sleeping hours. What kind of person am I? Did I let her die? Could I have tried harder? If my feelings are so powerful, is it best not to feel? One thing I know: I am never going to wish for anything ever again.

In the final analysis, Margaret did "get me," as this experience, combined with others, resulted in years of cries in the night and terror in the dark.

Section 4
The Wonder Years, 1963–1966

14
Out of Nowhere, 1963–1965

My strategy for survival is to perfect the art of the invisible. *I will be safer if I go unnoticed . . . if I do not draw attention to myself.*

I am already partially invisible, so it doesn't take a lot of effort, and it feels like action on my part. I am doing something proactive. It is important to me to feel that I am taking the initiative to move forward and doing something to protect myself. If not always successful, it is the best I can do.

After Margaret drowns, her children return to their grandparents to live. Patsy meets her future husband, gets pregnant, and marries. I am now David's protector.

My father again advertises in "The Lonely Hearts Club," looking for a lonely heart. He finds one in Kentucky. A single mother, Dorothy, responds to his ad. Shortly after they talk on the phone, Dorothy and her two children—Rebecca, age thirteen, and John, age twelve—join us in California. Calvin and Dorothy marry in February 1963, six months after Margaret's death. At thirty, she is robust—well, actually obese. Dorothy is a formidable presence walking through a room; she fills up the couch and the room. She wears her hair pulled back and tucked into a severe bun at the back of her head. Her dark eyes are folded into her cheeks. She wears flowing, sleeveless dresses that reach below her knees, leaving her large, muscular legs visible as she walks across the room. Dorothy and her children move into the house in Sacramento, and then my father gets a new job in a different town.

We move from the suburbs out to farm country north of Sacramento. Dorothy is Pentecostal. Religion enters our lives, as well as greens and grits. Miles from town, we live in a dilapidated farmhouse, a large oak tree in the yard with a tire swing. The road is straight and empty in all directions. Life consists of school, chores, homework, staying in my room, and going to church. I have just turned fifteen and am a junior in high school. It is four months until I am a senior. I already know I will get a better job if I have a high school diploma. I take typing and math classes so I will be ready to work when the time comes. School is still my safe place; I still never miss school.

I am in the bedroom I share with Becky when I hear Dorothy call out, "Diana, get out here. Your father wants you."

"I'll be right there," I call out as I rise up from the bed, put my book on the pillow, slip my shoes on, and head for the door.

What does he want?

I walk into the kitchen and see my father at the kitchen table. No expression shows on his face. He looks haggard, as if he is tired or defeated.

As I catch his eye, he says, "Your mother has sent tickets for you and your brother to fly to England. You are going to live with her." He speaks in a gruff monotone. "Get your things together; you will be leaving on Wednesday. Your mother will pick you up in London."

He does not provide any context. There is no discussion, just a flat statement. Wednesday is in three days! We have not lived with our mother for ten years and have not seen or heard from her in the five years since we went to Switzerland. We don't even know where she lives.

The revelation from Calvin is over in less than sixty seconds but not the excitement it generates. I am stunned and lightheaded. I keep turning over his words in my mind to make sense of them. I am rooted in the doorway, trying not to show the wonder I am feeling inside. *Three days!* I can't quite grasp what I just heard.

Three days! Did he just say that? Did I imagine it? Looking at his stony face and clenched mouth, it is hard to tell if he actually said anything.

I remind myself, *He said it and I heard it; it must be true!*

So soon. A lifetime away.

I have not seen or heard from my mother since the trip to Switzerland. Not since she told me that the reason she left us, my siblings and me, with my father was because he was "too violent," and she couldn't live with him. That last day is a vivid memory, tucked away but not forgotten. I had been fantasizing possible reasons: she might have been ill, or couldn't take care of us for another reason.

You left us with Calvin because he was too violent for you to live with? I looked at this person, my mother, unable to voice out loud the thundering thoughts rolling around inside my head. This is the person I wanted to love and who I wanted to love me. *What kind of mother is she?*

I didn't ask my mother any questions. My mother is not someone who will protect us when she has the opportunity to do so. It has been an oft-repeated choice and lesson. I still want her to love me; I'm just not sure she can. *Why would she have us now? What will we do about school? I am almost a senior.* David is twelve and has a long way to go with his own set of tribulations.

What do we need to pack? Does she really want us? What kind of mother will she be? Does she love us? How did this happen?

I keep repeating the same questions over and over in my mind, without answers. *Why is Calvin letting us go now?* I am dumbstruck.

"Really?" I finally reply, trying to keep the excitement from my voice. "We are going to England?"

"Yes," he says, "for two years—that's all."

I ignore the resolve in his voice. *Two years is a lifetime.*

Two years, I keep repeating to myself in a whisper.

I don't know what living with my mother will be like. I do have happy memories of her when I was small, and living with her has to be better than the life we are living with Calvin. Even though she has abandoned us before—twice—this is for two years. That's a lot. I'm sure Calvin hears the excitement and lack of reservation in my voice and sees the look of wonder on my face.

As I look around my room, I see there really isn't much to pack: a few articles of clothes, pants, a dress and a sweater, a coat, a spare pair of shoes, and my books. I stuff the clothes into a duffel bag and help David pack his. My favorite books, *The Odyssey* and *The Iliad*, are in a small pouch for the plane, and I am carrying a photograph of Patsy and John.

On Wednesday, I say a brief goodbye to Becky, John, and Dorothy. I am not sad to be leaving. A silent Calvin drives the two hours to the airport in San Francisco and coordinates with the airline to make sure that David and I board the plane.

As he turns away to leave, he says, "Two years, that's all," and walks away down the terminal, leaving us with a woman from the airline.

We are going to an unknown place, to live with a mother we have not lived with for over a decade. We have never met Stanley, her husband, and hardly know Jamie, our half brother, who was a small boy when we saw him in Switzerland. We don't know if she will be there when we land in London. It doesn't matter; we are away.

What does she look like? Will I recognize her? Does it matter?

We are left to ponder our future on the long, seemingly endless flight from San Francisco to London.

"What do you think will happen, sis?" David asks.

I am his protector. "I don't know, but it will be all right," I say, sounding positive. I am not entirely sure this is true but want to reassure him (and me). "She wants us to come. We'll manage; I'll be there to look after you. Besides," I add with an upbeat note, "it will be an adventure."

"It can't be worse than the way we have been living," my wise twelve-year-old brother comments.

A reassuring thought. David is right. We are flying off into uncharted waters but with anticipation. Life can only get better. I hope.

When we arrive in London, the flight attendant shows us where to get our suitcases and how to go through the entry and customs line. She points to the left.

"Your mother will meet you on the other side of those double doors."

After our passports are stamped, we exit through the big green double doors. I see my mother out of the corner of my eye, still recognizable, although she is a little heavier. Her brown hair falls around her face, a big smile in her eyes and on her mouth. She is wearing a blue linen dress and low platform shoes, and she waves as we come through the exit door.

"Hello, darlings," she says. "It is so good to see you."

That's promising. Darlings? Then I wonder, *What do I call her? Mother, Mum, Mummy, Geraldine?*

Ever the diplomat, I say, "Hello, Mum. Thank you for having us." She had been my mummy once, a long time ago.

She hugs me, an unaccustomed experience, and then turns to hug David.

"Let's go catch our train and go home," she says excitedly.

David and I look at each other and grin. We have never been on a train; this is indeed an adventure.

"I'm sorry," my mother says. "It is nine more hours by train to where we live in Cornwall in the town of Penzance."

As far as I'm concerned, this is just fine. It puts us even farther away from California than we are already. We are going "far and away" from life with my father . . . the farther, the better.

The train station is immense. People hustle about, moving to and from different tracks. Trains are going across England to the north, west, and south. People are traveling somewhere, hurrying and bustling with trailing bags and children. Feet scurry down the side of the track to the trains. Train arrival and departure times blare over the loudspeakers.

"Down here, on Track 1," my mother says. "This is the train to Cornwall. We are in the fourth car, right down there."

I see other passengers hurrying to find their cars and compartments. I hear two short wailing sounds.

"Hurry, darlings," my mother says again. "The whistle means the train is about to leave, and we don't want to miss it."

We find our car and compartment number and climb up the three short steps to the train car. There is a bar to hold onto as we pull up the bags and ourselves into the train. My mother says to push the green button on the side, and the door will open. I reach up and push the button, and the door slides open onto a narrow hallway with compartments on one side and windows on the other.

"Here's Compartment 4," my mother says. "Put the suitcase overhead or under the seat. We will be leaving soon."

There is a big window, and I can see out of the train from either one of the two red upholstered bench seats in the compartment. I pick the one on the left, placing the duffel under the seat and the smaller bag with my books in the overhead bin. I help David with his things. I hear the long wail of the whistle as the train lurches forward, moving slowly out of the station.

At first, looking out the window, I see dingy houses with small yards and laundry hanging out, flapping in the wind. The trees are bare of leaves, and it appears dreary and cold. Slowly we leave the city, and I see the green and velvet countryside flashing past as we speed across the landscape toward the southern tip of England. Land's End, as south as one can go in England, on the edge of the sea. I can hardly imagine what that will be like. I was small the last time I was by the sea—as it happened, in Cornwall with my mother.

Instead of wondering, I focus on what I can see. There are cattle, sheep, horses, green pastures, funny stone fences, hedges that divide the fields, villages in the distance, and an occasional farmer in the fields. The sky holds many-layered patterns of gray, white, and blue.

"Shall we go and get something to eat?" my mother asks.

"Yes, please," we both respond.

As we walk along the corridor, David and I reach out our arms to the side, touching for balance in case of a sudden jolt. The dining room is two cars down, so we must walk along another corridor before we get to the restaurant. The train cars sway back and forth, the tracks singing their clickety-clack sounds as the wheels run along the rail lines. We sit at a table with napkins, several pieces of silverware, glasses for water, and cups for tea. This is not the first time I have seen things like napkins and teacups on the table. I saw them in Switzerland years earlier, so it is not a surprise to me but more of a surprise for David.

"Here, David. This is your napkin," I say as I shake out mine and place it in my lap. David is a quick learner.

"Taste the tea to see if you like it. You might want sugar and milk. Let's look at the menu and see what there is to eat."

"I'm starving," he says.

"Order anything you like." Our mother laughs. "I am sure you are hungry." She seems genuinely happy to see us.

David and I decide on a meal of fish and chips, food we haven't eaten since Switzerland. It is a novelty to eat in a restaurant, especially one that is swaying gently back and forth as the train speeds along, bringing us to our new life.

"Where are we going?" I ask as I take a sip of water.

"After we leave London, we travel past Reading. There will be a long space, and then we will see Plymouth, Truro, and on into Penzance," my mother explains. "Cornwall is at the very southern tip of England. Penzance, where we live, is the largest town, with fishing villages dotted across the coastline on both sides."

When we finish our fish and chips, we walk down to our compartment, the train moving faster but still rocking gently on the tracks.

Before we go to sleep, my mother explains that she, Stanley, and Jamie live in a pub/hotel.

What will that be like? I am soothed by the steady rhythm of the train wheels rolling along the tracks.

Cornwall sounds very different from the ramshackle farmhouse on the outskirts of Vacaville, the place we just left. I am simply happy to be where I am in this moment, my eyes taking in the beauty of the country, the train lulling me to sleep. David chatters with our mother. I don't know what to expect from my mother, but we are here. I decide not to worry about that for now. I slowly drift off to sleep.

"Wake up, Diana. We will be arriving soon," my mother says.

The train station looms ahead. Delayed at Plymouth during the night, we arrive in Penzance later in the morning than expected. Mother explains that Stanley will be at the train station to meet us and take our bags back to The Dock. There isn't enough room in the van for our luggage and the three of us.

When the train stops, we unload our bags onto a cart and push it out the big station doors into a parking lot. We see a man across the parking lot, leaning up against a white van with his arms crossed. When we come out, my mother points to the van.

"There's Stanley."

To the man she says, "Stanley, this is Diana and David. Say hello."

"Hello," he says, and turns to Mother. "It's about bloody time! I'm late. I'll see you at The Dock." To David and me he says, "Put those bags in the back of the van. I'm late." We lift the bags into the back. He shuts the door, gets into the van, and drives off. Not exactly welcoming. A preview of things to come?

From the train station, my mother, David, and I walk along the waterfront, marveling at the boats, fishermen, and seagulls flying overhead. The wind is brisk and cold, gusting off the Atlantic, as we trudge along the dock road. It has taken almost eighteen hours to arrive in Penzance; we are tired but happy.

My mother explains that The Dock is located across the waterfront at the end of the quay. The first inkling that living in Cornwall is going to be unusual is when I fully realize we will be living by the sea. As we walk along the front, I see fishing boats in the harbor. I glance to the right and can hardly believe my eyes. A castle rises from the sea, on an island in the middle of the bay. It's astonishing!

"Look at the castle in the water, David!"

We don't just live by the sea; the sea is practically outside our front door. The wind is cold, coming off the February sea, brisk and exciting.

By the sea!

As we round a corner, I see a sign that says, "The Dock Hotel." *This must be it.* I look up at the two-story, granite-surfaced building with two window fronts, a central doorway, and a large awning. Tall green and white letters, announcing "The Dock Hotel," are blazoned across the front doors of the building. There are three sets of windows across the second floor where the hotel rooms are.

From the front steps of The Dock, I turn and look across the bay to Mousehole, a small village, and St. Michael's Mount, the thirteenth-century castle I saw as we walked along the waterfront. The castle's medieval towers rise into the sky on top of the promontory. There is a cobblestone road that leads from the village to the castle. My mother explains that when the tide comes in, the road is covered by water. At high tide, the only way to the island is by a small boat. I smell the strong, briny scent of the sea and fish from the boats bobbing on the water. Seagulls fly in circles above the harbor, whirling overhead and searching for food. I am enchanted.

The Dock Hotel is on the quay, where the fishing boats moor and the tourist boats come in and out, taking tourists to the Scilly Isles. The "Scillies," islands off Penzance, are famous for hiking and the fields of flowers the islanders grow. My mother explains there is a small pub garden at the back of the hotel and another small public garden beyond that. Across the road from the gardens is the town's saltwater swimming pool. There is a promenade that follows an estuary for a mile to the fishing village of Newlyn.

I feel like Dorothy in Oz; I am definitely not in Kansas anymore. Although I have not clicked ruby-red slippers, here I am—we are—in another world, a land of Oz. I know instantly that I will love this place. It feels magical.

My mother opens the door and rushes down the hall, talking over her shoulder.

"I'm late. I have to do the till before the bar opens. Come in and ask Betty for a soda. Come up to the back room when you are done." She continues talking as she hurries down the hall. "Stanley has unloaded the suitcases and is in the bar getting ready for opening. I must go too. I'll orient you to the hotel and your work at tea. Go ahead and settle in." She disappears around a corner. "It's down the hall and slight right, and then left is the door to our sitting room."

Welcome to Cornwall. This life will indeed be different. I know I will love living by the sea. I wonder about living in a hotel.

Such rosy words cannot be applied to my relationship with my mother and stepfather. Things do not turn out quite as simple as they seemed upon our arrival in London. However, I think it will be better than where we have been living with Calvin in America.

This is the place where I begin to discover myself.

15

Snaggletooth and Thunder Thighs

David and I stand under the awning at the front door, peering down a long, wide hallway. Mother and Stanley have disappeared. We look at each other, and David asks, "What does 'settle in' mean?" All we can see from the front step is a long hallway.

"Hello, my loves," a woman's voice in a strange accent calls out from midway along the hallway.

"Does she mean us?" David says.

A woman leans over the hallway bar and says in what we will learn is a strong Cornish accent, "Welcome to Cornwall. Let's see you, then. Come up here so we can have a look." She laughs as her hand reaches out over the top of the bar, beckoning us to join her down the hall.

"My name is Betty," she says. "We've heard a lot about ye and are curious now to see these American children. Come up here and let us see you," she repeats.

In her forties, tall and thin with short, discolored, bleached-blonde hair, yellowed teeth, and a cigarette hanging out the side of her mouth, Betty continues to wave us forward. With bright-blue eyes and an easy smile, she serves the regulars who come into The Dock for their pint of Guinness or a drink of gin and tonic.

"I saw your mother go up the top. She'll be down in a minute. 'Ere, let me tell you how it works," she says kindly.

David and I walk up the hall and stop at the bar door. "I'm Betty," she says again. "I'm the barmaid, and who might you be?"

"I'm Diana, and this is David."

"Well, hello to you both. Let me get you a soda, and I'll tell you about the pub," she says with a quick nod and a wink, cigarette smoke spiraling about her head. "On the pub side, where I am, is where the locals from these parts sit to have a pint of beer or a whiskey or a gin at lunch or after work or dinner. Children are not permitted on the bar side, only in the lounge. Smoking is allowed only in the bar. No smoking in the lounge."

I don't smoke, at least not yet, so this admonition doesn't apply to me.

I peer over the half door and see into the space behind the bar. Alcohol bottles are lined up along the back wall, and three beer barrels are lined up under the long, inner bar. Tall beer pulls sit above the barrels with a tray underneath to catch any spillage. Betty points out the nautical decorations on the walls, reminders of Stanley's youth as a merchant seaman. Few customers are in the bar and no one is in the lounge. Stanley dries bar glasses on the other side of Betty in the inner pub side. A strong smell of stale, spilled beer and cigarette smoke floats in the air. The walls are paneled in dark wood with benches along the wall and several bar stools up against the wall-to-wall bar.

On the other side of the entryway is the lounge where customers sit more openly at tables, a space that doubles as the breakfast room and lunchroom. Children are welcome in the lounge but not permitted alcohol.

"See that platform there in the corner?" Betty points across the hall. "That's where your mother sings. She loves to sing, that one does. The Cornish love their drink and singing the auld songs. Your mother has the voice."

Chattering on, Betty explains there are three steps ahead, and then if we turn right at the end of the hall to a small alcove where the telephone is, there is a small ledge where my mother checks the hotel guests in and out. Beyond that, stairs lead up to the hotel bedrooms. There are five bedrooms and a bath upstairs in the hotel part of the building. On the left are the "family quarters," including a living room with electric fire, table, couch, and a small television. There is a little pie-shaped room in the corner, a pantry, and a long, narrow kitchen. At the back of the kitchen, steep stairs lead up to the attic bedroom.

"You'll see soon enough that your mam has a green thumb. Lovely flower baskets in the spring," Betty continues as she motions up the steps to a door that leads out into a small garden. Pub guests sit in the garden when the weather is warm.

My mother sings and gardens! This is news. What else will I learn about her while we are here?

Just then, my mother, having changed her clothes, comes out of the family quarters and shows us where we will be sleeping.

"Diana, for now your bedroom is at the top of the stairs on the right in the hotel section."

This room is known as a "single," the smallest of the hotel rooms. The plan is that in the summer, I will move my things out so that the room can be rented to paying guests. For now I have "a room of my own." David is to sleep in the small, pie-shaped room off the living room in the family quarters, and Jamie, in the attic bedroom on the other end of the house where Mother and Stanley sleep. In the summer, David will move up to the attic, and I will have the small boxlike room off the living area.

"Settle in. We will have tea and talk later," my mother says. "I have to work in the bar now."

She leaves David and me in the family living room wondering what to do next. Jamie sits on the couch with a sullen look. He is not sure what to do with us. Two older children, his brother and sister, have suddenly been thrust into his life. Jamie is no longer an only child, and we are Americans . . . a curiosity to all. He glares at us as we join him on the couch, waiting for our mother to reappear. She has told us we are not allowed in the bar when alcohol is served.

Finally, at 2:00 p.m., my mother comes up from the bar.

"You can go for a walk along the promenade, if you like," she tells us. "Just out the back door, across the small garden and past the swimming pool. I am going to take a nap, and then we will have tea and a chat at four o'clock."

My mother explains that afternoon tea is an English tradition. Generally, tea is served as a midafternoon holdover until a more substantial dinner in the evening.

David and I go for a walk along the promenade. We exit out the back garden of the pub and walk past the saltwater pool, along the bay that fronts onto Newlyn Harbor.

As we walk, I again feel a sharp breeze from the water on my skin, chilly on my face and neck. I love the smell of the briny salt water and the sound of the gulls noisily searching for fish as they skim over the water. These sounds are music to my ears. Off in the distance is a village and a small harbor with more fishing boats. When I realize we are surrounded on three sides by water, I feel a surge of excitement. I immediately feel connected to this place . . . at home despite the early awkwardness at The Dock. This feeling is inexplicable, surprising. I have been by water before, but there is an almost magical air about this place. Walking to Newlyn, we see the shape of the village ahead and to the right, the town of Penzance rising up the hill. Penzance is the biggest town in this part of Cornwall. The tide is out, exposing the pebble and rock beach below the promenade.

"Another time we will go down and look for creatures in the rock pools," I tell David. "We have lots of time. Two years."

When we reach the end of the promenade, we turn around and walk back to the hotel and sit in the living room, waiting for my mother. The kitchen maid brings in a tray with tea and biscuits, which we call cookies.

Without much fanfare, my mother comes in from the bar, sits down, and talks about what is next.

"On Monday, we will enroll David in school, but you, Diana, are too old for school in England."

"No school?" I look up at her in surprise.

In England, at fifteen, students take a test to determine whether their future is a grammar school and university or entering the workforce, which may mean technical college. I am fourteen and have not gone through the English school system; I do not qualify for grammar school. My future is a technical school or to enter the labor force.

"Diana, you must work for your keep," Mother says.

Ah, the punch line.

My duties will include being a waitress and a hotel maid. I am to clean the lounge each morning from the previous evening's customers, set up the breakfast tables, prepare and serve breakfast, clean the dishes, do the shopping, make up the hotel beds, clean the hotel bathroom, and do whatever else is necessary to run specific parts of The Dock. David will help clean and restock the bar after school. My mother keeps the books, does some cooking, schedules the rental of the rooms, and serves in the bar in the afternoon and evening.

"After your work is done, you are free to do what you want," my mother says.

I won't actually get paid; I'll be earning David's and my keep—a small allowance for necessities.

I slowly figure out that "free labor" or "paying for ourselves" is how my mother sold our presence to Stanley. He has made it clear that he is not excited about our being here. My father once told us Stanley had not wanted my mother to keep us with her ten years earlier when she abandoned us, and it feels like he doesn't want us now. For unknown and mysterious reasons, my mother has prevailed in this instance. We are here, but with conditions.

My day starts at 5:30 a.m. The Dock Hotel is a bed and breakfast.

In addition to breakfast for hotel guests, we also advertise breakfast to the public. We put a sign out on the quay. We serve tourists who come down to board boats for the Scilly Isles or to fish for mackerel in the waters off the quay. We are busy even in the winter months. I worry about climbing the steps to the kitchen and coming back down to the breakfast room with full trays of food.

Breakfast is standard English fare of bacon, eggs, fried tomatoes, and toast, and sometimes baked beans.

"Can you get me another rack of toast and more tea please?" says a guest.

"Of course. I will be right back," I cheerily reply, hoping I won't trip on the stairs coming down, as I am prone to do.

The boat for the Scillies leaves by 10:00 a.m., so there is time to clean the dishes, make the beds, and clean the bathroom upstairs before the lunch crowd starts. While my mother is in the bar or off somewhere in town, my job is to make sandwiches and serve lunch. The most popular item and the easiest to make is the "Ploughman's Special," a Cornish specialty consisting of a chunk of sharp white cheddar and crusty bread, with small round pickled onions on the side. Another favorite is the Cornish meat pasties, a meat-and-vegetable pie folded in half, the dough pinched together to hold the meat and vegetables inside. Pasties are routine pub food and can be eaten cold or hot. My favorite is a hot pasty.

The smell of pasties fresh from the oven makes my mouth water, and when the local baker delivers the day's order of freshly baked, crusty, buttery pasties, I anticipate the crust melting in my mouth. If I'm lucky, there isn't any gristle in the meat.

The physical risks associated with cleaning the bedrooms and bathroom upstairs are less than serving as a waitress. There are fewer opportunities to trip and send a tray of breakfasts flying down the hall or into the lap of a startled customer. This has happened more than once. I am a clumsy when negotiating stairs with a full tray of breakfasts.

"You are clumsy Diana," is Stanley's usual retort if I do something he thinks I should be criticized for. "Probably those thunder thighs of yours. They put you off-balance," he says in a mean voice loud enough for all to hear.

A hurtful comment from Stanley is not unusual, especially remarks focusing on my physical attributes.

I do have hefty thighs, the same physiology as my mother, but I don't need Stanley to point it out. It is clear his spiteful words are meant to demean—more often when "in his cups," or drunk, which is frequent. He makes fun of me with the regulars in the bar when it is not busy, commenting on my physical appearance and capacity.

"Clumsy clot," he calls me, laughing with the patrons. It is a common Cornish insult. He embarrasses me by calling out to all in attendance, "And look at that snaggletooth! I thought all Americans had perfect teeth." He laughs and encourages the bar customers to laugh as well. This is a reference to an embarrassing dental condition. I still have one of my baby teeth as a front tooth. It is half the size of my other primary front tooth, and the enamel is scored. I am embarrassed but helpless to do anything about it other than manage by not smiling, speaking through half-closed lips, and holding my head down. Some kind of put-down is the most typical response I receive from Stanley, and my tooth and thighs draw his attention.

"Don't take no notice of the bloody idiot. He is a ninny," Betty says in an aside. "Just ignore him, my duckling; he will go on to something else. He always does." She is trying to be kind, but the "kicker" gives me pause for thought.

"You remember the tale of the ugly duckling?" she asks. "The one that went on to be a beautiful swan? You have the makings of a swan, me hansome," she slurs in a thick Cornish accent, obviously in her cups. "Just hold onto that."

I am an ugly duckling, even to the barmaid.

Betty, who can handle being a bar mistress, is trying to be kind.

She has good intentions, and she looks after my interests when she can. She makes me a cold Cornish "shandy" of lemonade and sparkling water as I ponder the ugly duckling comment.

"I'm sure the pasties contribute to my thundering thighs." I sigh as I sip my drink. I do love pasties.

It doesn't take long to discover another way I will be useful in my mother's life.

On Tuesdays and Thursdays, in her high voice she calls out, "Diana, be ready in ten minutes to go to the market and butcher's. We can have some mother-daughter time." She says this loud enough for Stanley, who is in the bar, to hear. To Stanley she says, "Diana and I are off now to do some shopping and have tea. We'll be gone a few hours."

"Come on, Diana; let's go."

I follow behind her, out the door, and up the hill toward town.

When we get to the top of Market Street, my mother leans over and says in a quiet voice, "Meet me here in two hours; we'll go back down together. I have some errands to run." As she moves off around the corner onto York Street, she adds, "Don't be late."

So much for "me and mum" time. I realize I am her excuse to cover for an affair with one of the local fishermen. *She doesn't want to spend time with me. She is using me.* It is sad but somehow not surprising.

It is left unsaid but understood that I will not share our parted ways on the high street. The illusion of togetherness must be maintained by returning to The Dock together. My mother carries some of the vegetables I purchased at the grocer's. In addition to being the hotel maid, waitress, and general gofer, my purpose is to provide cover for her trysts in town. This doesn't exactly make me feel that my mother loves me as a person, but I love the freedom of roaming around for several hours on my own. I didn't start off with high expectations.

On my solitary wanderings in town, I reflect on my life at The Dock and realize there is a new front to manage.

In America, Calvin attacked me physically or failed to protect me, but he did not directly attack my self-esteem. I never felt love, so I didn't expect it; it wasn't a question. Here, I had hoped for love from my mother, indeed yearned for it.

Instead, she is assuaging her guilt and using me to further her purposes . . . The opposite of my father, Stanley attacks verbally, not physically. I live in a flip-flopped world.

Who orchestrated this scenario? What happened to Beaver Cleaver, Donna Reed, and *Father Knows Best* families? I didn't get one of those in America. *Doesn't look like I'm going to get one here either.*

In contrast, David seems to be thriving from the change. He goes to school, makes friends, and roams around the town having fun. I learn later that he is developing a reputation with the young ladies, this blond, engaging American boy. I don't have to worry about him. Stanley leaves him alone, and he is enjoying his new freedoms.

Despite what might seem to be an inauspicious start, these years living in Cornwall are a pivotal time. These two years save my life. I have much to be grateful for.

Section 5
Emerging from the Chrysalis

16
Freedom and Friendship

I try to think of her as my mother, but I cannot relate. The chasm between us is too vast, too deep.

I knew it in my heart when I was ten, but it took a few more years to ken.

I want her to love me, but I don't think she does. Or, if she does, it is not a love that I understand. It is the yin and yang of our relationship. My mother and I never quite connect. We did at one time, when I was a child, I think. I have fond memories, but those are overshadowed by what came afterward. I learned early that I could not trust her to protect me.

Maid and waitress chores are done for the day, and I am free to do whatever I want—within limits. The absence of supervision is delightful, and I begin to spread my wings. When my mother does oversee my time, her lessons are of deceit and lying to cover up what *she* is doing. I understand the deceit part, but not the straight-up lying—any chance of that was beaten out of me by my father long ago.

I don't mind the work. If that is the price of freedom, so be it. It is not what I want from her, but I have to think she gives what she has to offer. I don't have high expectations. It is enough that I live here in Cornwall. My spirit soars.

My mother takes me to the dentist to get my snaggletooth pulled and a replacement prosthetic made. The new tooth slips a little, making a slight hissing sound when I use words with "s" sounds. I am still self-conscious, but it is oh-so-much better now that I have a "normal" tooth when I smile. I am grateful for the upgrade. It has removed one of Stanley's taunts; he can no longer call me "snaggle-tooth." He still makes full use of "thunder thighs" and "stupid get," a Cornish insult. Despite his meanness, I am developing more self-con-fidence. I ignore him as much as I can. He never touches me; he isn't violent, at least physically. He is mean and demeaning. I don't know why; I've done nothing to him. I stay out of his way.

I find many amusements to watch and wonder at. I love these solitary times, a novel experience for me. I am captivated and exhil-arated. I explore the town and the countryside. I walk up the old cobblestone road to Main Street, down to the promenade to walk along the cove, up the road to Newlyn, and into the town gardens. I look in the shops and stop for Cornish ice cream. I walk along the high street, admiring the shop window displays, and wander down to watch the train come into the station. I watch the fishing boats coming into the harbor with the tide. I sit on the seawall and gaze over at the castle on St. Michael's Mount and wonder about olden days. I am also listening to the strident chatter of the seagulls, noisy but soothing, as they circle overhead, searching for a stray fish from the fishermen as they wash down their boats from their morning catch. I am happy in this place.

Occasionally, I capture my mother's attention. She thinks she has to "do" something with me or for me, such as teach me manners, how to dress, how to eat; provide me with the right education; and make me understand what "class" I am from . . . my place in life. On this day, the right thing from her perspective is for me to "mingle" with the "right sort."

"Diana, the mayor's daughter is coming later today to see if you would like to go for a walk," she says. "Josephine is a nice girl and from the right class. You should get on," she continues, as if class is what makes people relate to each other.

My mother encourages me to make friends with the children of doctors, teachers, the mayor, or councilmen. They are "our" kind, the "right" kind, she explains in her best well-bred Scottish voice—a woman who daily serves alcohol to working-class Cornish locals.

I make excuses for her. *She has no idea where I come from, my life in America with Calvin.* No matter how many times I think this, I know she knew. She was married to Calvin for nine years and created four children with him. She lived in America with him. Of course, she knew.

Perhaps she is trying to show me another side of life. I should give her the benefit of the doubt. I am cautious. She has not proved trustworthy in the past or present. In my other life, we do not mingle with the "right sort." We hardly mingle with *any* sort. It is an isolated existence.

I am confused by the contradictions not only in my old life but in this one, confused by my mother. *What planet does she come from?* I have no idea who my mother is; she is a mystery.

I wonder at this view of the world, at the irony of "my kind." My mother runs a bar, drinks copious amounts of alcohol, and has affairs on the side with a local fisherman. So I am confused by her view that I have a "kind," which is the upper crust in the local community—well, at least the middle crust. Class is relevant to the British.

I have a "kind," but I work as a waitress and maid to pay my mother room and board?

Sometimes I think my life is like an episode of *The Twilight Zone*, a program I watched a few times on television: weird and scary, with people in extraordinary situations trying to figure out which way to go.

If I think about it too much, it will make me laugh. I am coming from cow town to tea with the mayor's daughter. I am a waitress and a maid but must consort with the right sort.

I've never had a friend before, so I don't know what that is like. I'm open to the possibility. My relationships are with my siblings. My father's (or mother's) house is not one that I would bring friends to, even if I had a friend.

I don't really connect with Josephine. She is nice, but we don't "click." We are polite but not engaged. I guess I'm not her sort, or she is not mine. She is meeting me because she was asked to, not because she wants to. But the boon is that Josephine introduces me to the Winter Gardens, a local hangout for the teenagers of Penzance and neighboring Newlyn village—even farther along the coast if someone has a car. From my mother's perspective, since Josephine is the mayor's daughter and she goes dancing at the Winter Gardens, it must be an acceptable venue. It is here that I learn I love to dance, letting my body move without censure and letting go of worries and tension. It is here that I discover music in general. I have heard church music, country music, and pub music but not pop music. My introduction to the Winter Gardens is like an introduction to another self. I love to move my body to the beat of the music; I feel free from my clumsiness. I feel coordinated and fluid when dancing. The music reverberates through my head and limbs, flows out through movement as I gyrate across the floor. I am transported by the combination of sounds and the vibration of the music through my body.

Since it is 1965, girls stand around at the edge of the large dance hall and wait for boys to ask them to dance. Or girls dance with each other, and the boys cut in. Cornwall is in a remote part of England—change happens slowly. This is an ancient and pagan land, and what happens in other parts of the world is often slow to penetrate this isolated place. However, there is a Beatles craze here as elsewhere in the world, and youths dance the Twist and the Loco-Motion, slow dancing, and bebop. For an adolescent in South Cornwall, the Winter Gardens is the best place to be on a Friday night.

Everyone knows everyone else at the Winter Gardens. I am a newcomer. The word spreads that I am an "American."

"Right then, a Yank are ye?" one boy says.

"Yes, that's me, an American," I reply. "Would you like to dance?" It is a bold move on my part, but I'm glad to learn it is how things work. Girls can ask boys to dance, and of course, vice versa. I soon find myself in a circle with Lydia and Rosalie, who are fraternal twins.

"Hi, I'm Lydia. Who are you?"

"I'm Diana. I'm new here."

Lydia laughs. "That's obvious. Come over to our table and have a fizzy with us. We can get to know each other."

It is a welcome invitation. Lydia and I become best friends, and lots of times Rosalie is with us. A local group of young people—friends of the twins—invite me to join their group. It is a gift. After that, I don't quite become a local, but I am accepted. I am part of a group. I have friends, a special friend in Lydia.

On Friday nights, we go to the Winter Gardens, along with the other teenagers in the surrounding area. I walk along the promenade and meet Lydia at the bottom of her street. We walk together to the end of the road, where the Winter Gardens is located.

Fortunately, I am asked to dance a fair amount. A novelty, an American, I am a curiosity to the boys. I enjoy dancing, so the attention of the boys is OK with me, especially Richard, a heartthrob who glances my way on occasion. There is no lack of dancing partners. Lydia, a generous good friend, encourages her friends to dance with me. She is friends with some of the lads from Porthcurno, an international cable and wireless college located in a small village along the coast. They are young men from all over the world who come to Cornwall to study and are regulars at the Winter Gardens. They know we are fourteen or fifteen years old and are respectful of our age. They become our "protectors" and escorts for all things fun, as long as there aren't any older girls around. They treat us like younger sisters.

At the end of an evening of dancing, Lydia and I usually walk back along the promenade. I might stay over at her house and go back to The Dock in the morning.

It is an incredible year to discover freedom, my budding woman-hood, friendship, dancing, the wind and sea, and joy in life. If I didn't find a mother, I found so much else. I learned a long time ago that I can't have everything.

I am grateful for what I have.

17
The Plot Thickens

I don't remember how I learned that Lydia and Rosalie's father is in prison. I heard that he had been the police doctor but was convicted of conducting an abortion and sent away. I don't tell my mother. This detail is not a lie but a definite lack of disclosure, a reflection of lessons learned from my mother. I don't know what her view will be, but my guess is that my friendship with the Tellams would end before it started if my mother learned about Dr. Tellam. Right class, wrong behavior. She doesn't inquire and doesn't make the connection. I don't fill her in. I am learning well the lessons of concealment.

Lydia, my first real friend, is younger by a year, in her last year of middle school, preparing to take exams for grammar school. I am not in school, still learning "working skills" at The Dock Hotel. I am already squarely aimed toward emancipation, just not old enough to make it happen yet. I want to control my own life, not have others making decisions for me. I want to be free.

I'm grateful that Lydia is my friend. She is so practical, fun, and adventurous. Rosalie joins us in our adventures sometimes but is not always a sidekick. They are twins, but quite the opposite in appearance and personality. Rosalie is more subdued; she wears her long, straight reddish hair parted in the middle and is shorter than Lydia, more slender, with freckles across her nose. Lydia is taller and more rounded. Her short brown hair is cropped at her chin, and she has a mischievous gleam in her eye. We are compadres. Sometimes I walk across the promenade and up the road to the large row house halfway up the hill. The Tellams live on the other side of town, up in the terraces. Mrs. Tellam welcomes me at the door and always asks me about my day. We come into the house through the back door and up the stairs to the living quarters. Dr. Tellam's surgery, now unused, is on the ground floor and the bedrooms and living quarters on the two stories above. Lydia and Rosalie have their room on the top floor, a lovely attic space. I spend many hours there in inclement weather. We are often out on adventures when the weather cooperates. It is England, and the rain doesn't stop anyone. This is Cornwall; wind and rain are part of everyday life. It is the nature of the land. We are on the edge of the sea.

It is understood that we cannot meet at The Dock.

Lydia and I have many adventures that spring, summer, fall, and winter, and I have some of my own. I love to walk along the lanes outside of town to one of the villages in the surrounding area. I go to Lamorna, Newlyn, Mousehole, or catch a bus to Sennen Cove to sit and listen to the waves rolling in from the wild sea. Looking out, I know there are several thousand miles between me and the American continent. I sigh with relief.

I walk along the country lanes and enjoy the sunlight, the glimpse of fields through the stiles in the hedges, and the wildflowers—bluebells and buttercups—springing up out of the ground. I can hear the wind but not feel it within the confines of the narrow lane, protected by the hedges. It is different when I get out onto the headland. I'll both feel and hear the fierce wind then.

Sometimes I sing as I walk along the lanes, late '50s songs: Brenda Lee and others. I cannot really carry a tune, but I love to sing. There is no one to hear me except perhaps a stray farmer, and he likely thinks me "barmy." He will know I am the American girl. My brother and I are known in the town and the surrounding area because we are different—accepted but curiosities.

On one of my walks, I find the "Merry Maidens," a set of nineteen ring stones in a field on a hill, placed there by an ancient people of Cornwall. The "Pipers" are across the field. The legend is that nineteen maidens were out dancing on the Sabbath in the moonlight, probably practicing witchcraft or other pagan rituals, and they were turned to stone. This is a Protestant punishment tale. There are lots of places like this in Cornwall; its history is full of Druid rituals, shamanic magic, witchcraft, fairies, pixies, and elves.

When out among the fern leaves and foxglove, the Cornish girls sing, "*Fairy fair, fairy bright, come and be my chosen sprite,*" hoping a fairy will appear and grant them a wish.

I don't wish for things; I don't sing the fairy song. I am fascinated by magic but afraid of the idea of it. What if the dead can come back? It is a haunting question from my past.

Cornwall is an ancient and pagan place. Every village has someone thought to be skilled in magic and healing called a *pellar*, or white witch, especially if there is a spring-fed pool in or near the village. These beliefs, held down the ages, show up in local celebrations throughout the year.

Once, a group of friends went to the Witches Rock at Zennor to touch the rock nine times at midnight. This ritual was supposed to ensure against bad luck.

"Let's go," Lydia says. "I can use some good luck; my exams are coming up. We can ask the lads if they will drive us out and back." She is already thinking how we can accomplish our adventure.

I tell my mother I am staying at Lydia's overnight, failing to mention we have an adventure in mind. Mrs. Tellam is much more accommodating regarding adolescent adventures. Having grown up in Cornwall, she knows it is safe.

And it is. Mostly.

On May Day, we plan to attend the celebration in Padstow Common. Before midnight, hundreds of people gather below the clock tower in the village square.

"Come on, Diana! We want to be as near the maypole as we can," Lydia calls out. We wind our way through the crowd, and I catch up with her as she nears the central part of the square. The celebration begins by singing old Cornish songs. Then two different lines of dancers weave around the village, one group behind the Blue Oss (a mythical character), and one behind the Red Oss, representing males and females. Melodic accordion music interspersed with the wild beating of drums provides a rhythm for the dancing that goes on through the night. Eventually, the dancers arrive back at the center of town, where they wrap the many-colored maypole ribbons around the pole, laughing. May Day is basically an ancient fertility rite; there is lots of alcohol and revelry. I imagine there are lots of babies born the following February. But that revelry is not for Lydia and our friends. We leave after the winding of the maypole ribbons.

Looking back now, I marvel at how incredibly innocent it all was—perfect for me as I waded through discovering who I was beneath all the layers.

I don't drink. I tried a few times, but I don't like the taste of alcohol and definitely do not like the results of drinking. One hangover is enough to cure me of any interest in drinking copious amounts of alcohol, although I do enjoy a warm glass of honey mead on winter nights. When we are out in the cold and starry evenings, and near the monastery where the monks have the mead stills, we stop for a glass of hot mead. That lovely honey mead warms the soul inside and out. I've also been known to smoke a cigarette. My preferred brand is Gauloise, a strong, foul-tasting French cigarette.

In the summer, there is a Shakespearean festival at the Minack Theatre in Porthcurno. Sculpted out of the cliffs above Porthcurno Bay, the theater sits above the cliff and the sea below. The local bus takes us to below the cliff, and we walk up about forty granite steps cut out of the side of the cliff. The theater is carved from the rock with rows of circular stone benches looking down on the stage below. The backdrop to the stage is a balustrade and the ocean behind.

Lydia and I see *Romeo and Juliet* on that night of the full moon, and it is breathtaking, both the play and the moon. A huge sphere of yellow moon rides high in the sky—a yellow cream, a bright glow, and moonbeams on the ocean—rippling in the background, which is a perfect backdrop for the story of star-crossed lovers. It is a magical moment, learning about theater and the majesty of the sea and experiencing the joy of seeing moonbeams on the water from above, at the top of the cliff.

18

Learning to Ski

In early fall, my mother tells David and me that we are going on a holiday to Spain—to Malaga on the southern coast. We will drive up to Dover and catch the ferry to Le Havre, France, and then travel south to Spain. Malaga is a popular holiday resort for the British. My grandmother Reid will join us from Switzerland. I have to wear a dress for dinner. A bathing suit and shorts are the rest of my holiday wardrobe. I have pants and shoes for riding. We are going on horseback to the hills above Andalucía, through the groves.

On the first day at the resort, David and I walk along the boardwalk by the sea. I notice a sign advertising waterskiing lessons. Turning to David, I point my finger. "I want to do that. What do you think?"

"I think you will have to go into deep water," David replies. He knows about my fear of water.

It's an ocean, not a river. No eddies, no whirlpool. I remember why I am anxious in water over my head.

"I want to try it. I'm going to ask if I can."

My mother agrees that I can have a ski lesson. I listen carefully as the instructor tells me about going over the boat edge and slipping on the skis in the water. He explains how to position the skis so that I can get up out of the water when the boat begins to pick up speed in front of me. The idea is to pull me up so the skis skim across the top of the water.

I can do this.

I nod my head to acknowledge what he has explained. I am excited about trying. There is a moment of reluctance, of anxiety as the boat slowly moves out and away from the shore. I shake off my fear. *Maybe I'll be more graceful in the water. Relax, there is someone there to help you if anything happens. We are not that far out from the shore. You are a better swimmer now.*

I take a deep breath and brace myself as we arrive at the spot where I will have to go over the boat into the water.

Get a grip, Diana.

Even though I listened to and am trying to follow the instructions, I cannot coordinate keeping the skis in the right position, my hips in place, and my arms at the right angle. A few times I panic when I topple over and am pulled under the water in the boat's wake. Memories of the drowning flood my mind, resulting in a flash of terror. I shake my head and focus on the task in front of me. I am not going to let my anxiety and fear get in the way.

Unfortunately, feelings are not the key to success in skiing, which is much more about focus and coordination. I finally get up on the skis. By the time I succeed, my efforts have drawn a large crowd along the boardwalk. A raucous outpouring of shouts, whistles, and applause resounds off the promenade as I slowly rise up out of the water, my arms out in front, my spirit soaring. I have accomplished my goal! However, as the sound of clapping gets louder and louder, I look across to the boardwalk and realize they are clapping for me. I instantly lose focus and slowly sink into the sea. I decide I have had enough for one day and signal to the boatman that I am ready to get out of the water.

The crowd has dispersed by the time I climb into the boat, and we head for the shore. Laughing, David is there to greet me. "Way to go!"

The saga of my ski lesson has reached my mother and grandmother by the time I return to the hotel. I dress and join them on the patio. I see my grandmother's pursed lips, a sure sign of disapproval.

What have I done now?

It doesn't take long to find out.

"Well, Diana," my grandmother says. "The skiing lesson sounds embarrassing."

I look at her for a moment wondering if my mother will say anything. When she doesn't, I reply to my grandmother. "Not at all," I say with a glint in my eye, my chin raised high. "It took a while, but I accomplished what I set out to do. That's what is important."

My grandmother stares at me intently for a moment and then changes the subject, turning to David. "Tell me, David. What did you do today?"

His response warms my heart. "I watched my sister learn to ski. It was awesome!" We smile at each other, a sibling moment.

With attention diverted, I remember the afternoon and grin. I conquered my fear and reconfirmed to myself that determination pays off. I didn't set out to conquer fear, but that was the end result—a satisfying day.

19

Fleeing the Coop

When we return to England from our holiday, I approach my mother about a training program I heard about.

"Mum, I've been thinking about the future, and I think I might like to be a nurse."

My mother's brow wrinkles and she looks at me. "A nurse?"

"Yes," I say earnestly. "There is a training program at Penzance Hospital. At fifteen, in December on my birthday, I am eligible for the trainee nurse program."

It isn't so much that I want to be a nurse. In truth, my motivation is finding a way to move out of The Dock. I can be in an "apprentice" nursing program, take classes, live in the hospital dorm, and work on the wards. I am mostly interested in the part about living in the hospital dorms. My mother doesn't question me, agreeing that I can sign up for the nursing program without any resistance.

This is my first real taste of freedom. My dorm room at the hospital is the closest to the garden wall. It is the only room with windows that open outward, a perfect escape route for a late-night rendezvous. My room is the main route for the other girls on my floor to go out after curfew. Not that I went over the wall—I didn't, actually—but Matron doesn't believe me because of the muddy footprints on the rug in my room.

I am always in trouble for something. Once I dye my hair blonde, and it comes out green. No matter how much I wash my hair, the color just gets brighter. Fluorescent green hair, glowing under a very white nurse's cap. Matron is not amused.

On another occasion, the girls in my dorm are having a water fight, racing in and out of rooms, getting glassfuls of water to throw at each other. I am in the fray and dashing into my room, filling my glass with water. I have to juggle the glass and open the door to avoid spilling it. Unfortunately, Matron is on the other side.

"Miss English, whatever are you doing?" she demands in her high nasal voice, thick with a Cornish lilt.

"Nothing, Matron. Just having a sip of water." I quickly take a sip of water from the glass I am holding. "Can I help you?" I ask in my most courteous voice.

She isn't fooled by my cool act; I can tell by the look on her face. I am in trouble again.

I have almost reached the conclusion that I am not nursing material when I am assigned to the burn ward. The new patient on the ward, a young man, has third-degree burns over 90 percent of his body. He was caught in a boiler explosion. The smell of burned flesh is horrible, nauseating. I try to keep a smooth face when I help the head nurse change the boy's bandages, but I am horrified by what I see. He is in agony, and there is nothing I can do about it other than to try not to throw up in front of him. His eyes follow me. While I feel compassion, I just can't see myself taking care of the physical needs of patients. It is not my calling.

A final incident ends my nursing career. It is one of those late summer days I know will not last or come back again until next year. It is my day off, and I hike to the beach. I am standing on the roundabout at the edge of town when a car barrels around the corner. Before I can react, the car's side mirror strikes the back of my hand and wrist. My wrist is broken, requiring a cast, which interferes with my nursing duties. I am temporarily assigned to the X-ray room, which I find fascinating. I am taught how to develop X-rays and can look over the radiologist's shoulder when he reads the results. But the plaster cast on my arm, with various designs and decorations, is the death knell as far as Matron is concerned.

"Miss English," Matron says, "I think you might agree that you are not nursing material. Is that correct?"

"Yes, Matron. I agree."

Arrangements are made for me to go back to live at The Dock. Stanley must have thought he was rid of me, but I'm back again. I am a burr under his skin, an itch he can't get rid of. He doesn't do much except insult me and give me the stink eye. I suspect he is working on my mother in the background, telling her it is time for us to return to America.

I am older and wiser but back where I started. Well, not quite. I have had a taste of real freedom, and while I could have managed things better, it is enough to sustain me in forward momentum. When I return to The Dock, I immediately propose that I will pay rent from my wages. I will work somewhere else to pay for a maid and waitress at The Dock. I plan to get a job and bring in money to cover any costs to my mother from my return.

I find a job in the local hamburger place right away. Then I get lucky and find a job as a clerk in the feedstore at the bottom of the quay by the railway station. It is an easy walk across the front along the quay to the warehouse. My job is to tally sales and revenues in a journal. But in the summer, I have to move into the box room off the living area downstairs so my bedroom can be rented out to paying customers. I don't really care; I am mostly free. Living in a hotel isn't that much different from life as I had experienced it in the past: people moving in and out, changing places all the time. I don't have to do a lot of adjusting; it is the way it is.

20

Locked in the Tower or
Saving Me from Her Fate?

I come and go as I please within certain boundaries. I have a curfew, but I am not monitored in terms of where I go or what I do. If I want to do something after 10:00 p.m., I stay at Lydia's. My mother assumes I am doing innocent things, which I am . . . mostly. I am not interested in boys, at least not in sex. I don't trust males. I do notice boys and even have male friends among the Porthcurno lads for whom Lydia, Rosalie, and I are like younger-sister mascots. This is acceptable to my mother because the boys at the Porthcurno school are of the right social class, so I am allowed to mingle. A boyfriend is not what I want. I have just discovered freedom; I don't want to give it up. I am much more interested in exploring the countryside, sitting by the sea, and spending time with my friends, feeling free, although Richard is a very handsome guy.

It is late summer, and I make a new friend at the Winter Gardens. James, like me, is from a troubled family. He is not of the upper class, and we understand each other. He walks me back to The Dock sometimes in the evening. We sit on one of the benches on the promenade and talk about our hopes and dreams.

One Friday night in the fall of 1965, a group of us meet at the Winter Gardens. James, as usual, joins our group. We dance together, and James walks me home along the promenade after the dance. We share similar experiences of growing up in an abusive household; we have more in common than some.

I'm surprised when James stops along the promenade, turns to me, and blurts out, "Diana, I'm leaving Penzance and going north. I want you to come with me."

I am startled. It takes me a minute to find the right response. "It's lovely that you should ask, James. You know we are friends . . . but no more. I don't want to run away, and I don't want to leave Cornwall. Besides, I can't leave my brother. I thought you liked it here. Do you have to go away?"

"Yes," he says. "I have to leave. I'd like you to go with me. We can go away together and live in the north."

"No, James, I can't." *I don't want to.* "I am your friend, nothing more."

He is silent as we walk to the alley at the back of The Dock to say good night. "Think about it some more. I'm not leaving for a couple of days," he says, waving good night as he leaves to walk back along the front.

He is just impulsive; he doesn't mean it, I tell myself as I walk into The Dock. I don't think of him as a boyfriend. I put the conversation out of my mind and go up to bed.

On Saturday morning, I go about my usual morning activities, which include changing the bed linens and cleaning the bedrooms for a guest changeover. I supplement my room and board by working in the hotel on the weekends when help is needed.

I hear someone come up the stairs and enter the hallway. I look out the door of Room #3, where I have just stripped the bed of its sheets, and see my mother, her face flushed, barreling toward me. Her demeanor is fierce.

Too early for drinking. Perhaps she is going to her room at the end of the hall.

I watch her move along the hallway, her navy-blue dress already creased from sitting, snug around her ample stomach and hips. Her thin hair is flattened on one side where she has slept on it, her cheeks flushed, and her eyes glassy with what looks like determination.

What is this?

She hasn't said anything, and it is only a moment before she reaches me in the hall, takes my arm, and pulls me down the hall. "You are coming with me, missy." Her teeth grit a little as she takes charge of the situation, whatever it is. I've never seen my mother behave like this before, and I'm a little astounded.

What on earth is this about?

"Where are we going?" I ask, as she moves me along the hall toward the stairs.

"You'll see in a minute," she says. We turn down the stairs to the hall and move into the private living area, her hand tightly gripping my upper arm as if I would try to escape. We don't stop in the living room, though. She pulls me through the scullery and kitchen and points to the stairs to the attic room.

I look at my mother and ask, "What is going on?"

In response, she puffs up her shoulders and blurts out, "You are not running away! I am not going to let you make the same mistake I made, running off and getting pregnant."

She motions again for me to go up the stairs.

"Your young man left a note for you last night, urging you to come away with him. Someone heard him in the garden."

"You read my mail?" I ask in a quiet voice and then a louder voice. "He's not my young man, and he is not a bad person."

"There is a police manhunt. He'll not be coming back here." She lifts her finger again and points for me to go up the stairs.

I climb up the narrow, winding stairs to the room above the shed. It is a long room with a sloped ceiling and one small window in the west wall. There are three beds in the room—a double and two singles—as well as a dresser and some hooks for clothes. My mother and Stanley sleep here in the summer; the boys sleep up here in the winter.

Following me up the stairs, she continues, "Yes, the boy has a criminal background. Last night he stole a sports car from the garage at the end of the alley. We are lucky he didn't steal from here. But he did show up here yelling your name, calling for you to join him. Sometime during the night, he left you a note through the mail slot. There is no way I am going to let you run away with this boy. You will stay here, under guard, until he is caught."

"Wait! Don't you want to know what I have to say about this?"

"No, there is no discussion—you will not repeat my mistake!" Her tone is magisterial. "The boy will not be coming back here." In a firm but shaky voice, she repeats herself, "You'll stay up here until that boy is caught and in jail. There is no use thinking about escaping through the window. There is a policeman posted in the pub yard in case you try to get out. You stay put! Someone will bring you food and let you out for the bathroom." She locks the door behind her and descends the stairs.

I sit on the single bed and think about what just happened. I'm confused. *Jail? Policeman? What has James done? Why would she think I would run away with him?* Then I begin to understand. It sounds like she knows something about climbing out of windows and running away . . . because she ran away from her mother and got pregnant. *She cannot see me for who I am. She sees me only for who she is.*

The rest of that day and the next, I am locked in the tower awaiting the unknown. Indeed, there is only a small window that opens out onto the roof of the storage area below. I would have to climb out on the roof and drop down to the cobblestones below. I see a policeman standing guard near the garden gate. In the morning, my mother brings my breakfast and tells me the police are continuing to search for James. I see the policeman out of the corner of the window. He is indeed standing at attention, on guard.

I remain troubled that she never even asked me what I was thinking. She imprisoned me in the tower, placing a guard to ensure I don't run away and get pregnant.

Didn't she know about birth control? I suppose not.

It isn't until much later that I understand the multigenerational pattern my mother is so afraid of.

My grandmother had an affair. While my grandfather, a captain in the British Army, was stationed in India, his wife dallied in the Scottish Highlands with an Italian prisoner of war. In those days, officer prisoners were housed by the local population. Perhaps the affair could have been forgiven; Margaret and Gerald, my grandparents, had an arranged marriage. However, my grandmother got pregnant, producing a son and heir who was given the Paton Reid name. This male heir placed my mother on a lower rung in the family hierarchy and inheritance rights. My grandfather was humiliated.

My mother, then just seventeen, was outraged and rebellious. A daddy's girl, she was furious with her mother over the betrayal of her father. The impact was not limited to demotion in inheritance. She was sent south to boarding school. She attended Oxford's Girls' School and spent time with her maternal grandmother in London. This meant that my mother and her fellow schoolmates were near where American GIs were staged before or after entering the European war theater. My mother knew that her mother would disapprove if she dated an American GI. She met my father in 1944, near the end of the war, and was pregnant by January 1945. My grandmother, who hid her own illegitimate pregnancy, could not sweep my mother's indiscretion under the rug. Instead, she managed the situation as any well-bred matriarch would do.

My father was already married to his second or third wife (it is not clear) and was the father of at least one child. This was not an impediment for my grandmother. She swiftly arranged for my father to divorce his then-wife Faye and leave his son, Coy. My grandmother, with the wave of her rather full checkbook, paid Faye to travel from Oklahoma to Reno for a "quickie" six-week divorce, the goal being to legitimize my mother's pregnancy. She would marry my father, and the family name would remain untarnished. My siblings and I were born out of a relationship based on revenge, betrayal, and family pride . . . maybe some love, certainly some lust. They kept producing babies. These events influenced my mother's decision to lock me in the tower.

In the afternoon, I hear steps slowly climbing the stairs, and I am surprised to see my grandmother Reid enter the room. First, she and my mother are not on the best of terms. My grandmother doesn't like Stanley, and she has traveled from Switzerland for who knows what purpose. Since I don't have the friendliest relationship with my grandmother, I wonder why she is here. As usual, she has a dour expression. *Perhaps it is the bone structure.*

"Hello, Grandmother. Did you have a safe journey?" I ask, not knowing what else to say.

"Yes, thank you." Without further comment, she gets to the point. "I'm not here for a social call, Diana. I'm here to talk to you about this situation. Tell me what is happening here."

"I have no idea!" I insist. "Mother thinks I am going to run away with this boy, James. I just learned that he stole some money and a car and came looking for me. I don't want to run away with him!"

"Your mother seems convinced that you are planning to run away."

"No! James is a friend, but I don't want to go away with him. She didn't even want to hear what I had to say. She just made me come up here and stationed a guard so I couldn't leave.

A few days ago, he asked me to go away with him, and I said no. I told him I love living here and don't want to leave Cornwall. He has no reason to think I would go with him."

"Did you tell your mother this?" my grandmother asks.

"No. She didn't want to hear anything from me. She was certain I would get pregnant like she did when she was a girl. She said she wasn't going to let me make that mistake."

"Well, she *did* make a mistake; she has made a lot of mistakes. But I do agree with her that she has to protect you from a rash action that might have lifelong consequences. I'll speak to her and let her know what you have told me."

That evening my grandmother comes back and says, "You can come down. James has been caught and is in jail. You'll have to stay in the hotel this evening and can go to work in the morning. But be more careful with whom you choose to be friends."

Despite the ridiculousness of my mother's actions, this is the first time she has shown she cares on an emotional level. As misplaced as they are, in this case, her actions show a level of emotion I have not seen before. Unfortunately, while this event brings me a glimmer of understanding about my mother, it has the reverse effect on her. She finds it is more troublesome dealing with teenagers than she had bargained for, especially me. I'm sure Stanley is undermining our presence as well. She doesn't have the knowledge of her children that a parent has from raising them from infancy. She knows nothing about us, who we are, and doesn't know how to find out. She doesn't want to be responsible for us; she has done what she is going to do. We are on our own now. Her adventure into motherhood wasn't what she had envisioned.

21

Portents—A Walk in the Fog
or the Return of Fear

It is January 1966. I am sixteen and worried that the second anniversary of our arrival in England is closing in. No one has said anything about whether we are going back to America. I haven't spoken to my father for nearly two years. The last words he said to me, "Two years—that's all," echo in my head as I remember the day David and I left. I don't want to ask my mother for fear of the answer that she has decided to send us back. I should have expected what was to come, but I didn't.

There have been tensions with my mother and Stanley, but I am happy in Cornwall, and I want to stay. I am not thinking far into the future, but I know I don't want to leave now. I'm pretty sure David feels the same way.

It's Wednesday afternoon, and I am about to finish my workday at the Penzance General Supply Store. The store is mostly farmer-oriented: seeds, tools, and general hardware. My job is to keep track of inventory and sales. I post details into a log that is used to document the inventory process. Mrs. Penwith is the bookkeeping manager and my supervisor. She sits in a desk across from mine. She double-checks my work, but entering sales into the ledger is easy; I don't often make mistakes.

This is the job I found after my disastrous attempt at a nursing career. It suits me well for the moment as I think about what I want to do in the future. I am limited by the English educational system. Because I didn't go to grammar school here, I am locked out of many futures.

However, I'm learning skills, and I'm willing to work my way up. I don't want to go back to America, even though there may be more opportunities there. Not yet. Not now.

"I've finished up the books, Mrs. Penwith. I'll be off, if that's all right?"

"If you are walking home along the quay, wait up. I'll walk with you," she replies. In her forties, Mrs. P likes to walk to keep herself trim, and we sometimes walk together across the quay. Mrs. P and her husband live near The Dock Hotel and come to the pub on occasion.

"Not today. I'm going up the high street and across to my friend Lydia's house off Alexandra Road."

"Well, ye watch for the fog," she warns as I walk out the door. "This is one proper fog." She means it will be thick and heavy. "It's there on the horizon and will be coming into shore in a few hours."

"Thanks. I will," I reply cheerily, waving as I make my way out the door.

I see an ominous bank of fog across the harbor on the horizon. However, I soon forget the fog. My thoughts are on this evening. Lydia, Rosalie, and I are making plans for the weekend, and I'll have a chance to talk with Lydia about my worries. As my friend, she listens. From the store, I turn left a block over by the station. I walk up to Chapel Street so that I can go through the main thoroughfare and over to the terraces where Lydia lives.

The Tellams live in a three-story Victorian terrace house built with a lovely local creamy-colored stone. All the houses along the road are the same color and style, some larger than others. Lydia's house has canted bay windows on two levels that let lots of light in, a precious commodity in Cornwall, especially in the winter. Dr. Tellam's office, surgery, and reception area are on the ground level in the front. The main living rooms for the family are above on the first level, what I think of as the second floor, but they call it the first floor.

Upon arrival at the house, I walk through the iron gate, past the stone-and-hedge fence that lines the front of the house. There is a small yard, and a cobblestone path runs along the side of the house to the back door. Before I have time to knock, Lydia opens the door, saying, "I heard the gate."

"Up here in the family room," Rosalie calls out.

As I enter, I hang up my coat and scarf on a spare peg on the wall and climb up the stairs to the family room. There is a fire in the grate, and I walk across immediately to warm myself in front of the burning coals. "Brrr, it is cold and damp out there."

I welcome the heat creeping into my fingers and up the back of my legs as I stand by the fire. I'll soon be warm on the inside as well, full of laughter with friends. Lydia has brought in a kettle of tea, cups, sugar, and milk as well as Scottish butter biscuits, my favorite. As we make our tea, the three of us begin plotting a new adventure for the weekend. "Yes!" Rosalie exclaims. "The Winter Gardens. I'm hoping Brian will be there." She smiles. Lydia and I smile at each other as if we didn't know that.

"I want to hear the latest Beatles songs," says Lydia. Neither Lydia nor I have a boyfriend; we like to dance and see our friends.

Our plans for Saturday will depend on the weather and how much of her studies Lydia completes in the next few days. She has an important exam coming up that she must pass. I'm flexible. Other than checking on David, it doesn't matter whether I am at The Dock or not. I come and go within reasonable confines, and my mother has long accepted my friendship with Lydia.

"We are still planning the overnight on Friday," Lydia says.

"Yes, that's right. We can go to the Winter Gardens, then I'll stay over."

Staying over is something I do as often as I can, especially if we will be out late. Despite the absence of their father, the Tellam siblings and their mother are a family, and I am glad to be welcomed among them.

Startled by the door opening, I look up to see Lydia and Rosalie's older brother, Dave, coming in from his after-school job. His arrival means it's later than I thought. Time, as it often does at the Tellams', has slipped away.

"Oh! I need to go. It's late!" I say as I jump up, picking up my teacup to take back to the kitchen.

"Aye, be careful out there. The fog is getting thicker," Dave says.

Lydia announces that she will walk me to the end of the road, as she often does at the close of my visit. We bundle up and walk down the hill, talking. This is our quiet time to talk.

"I don't know what my mother is going to do, Lydia. I'm worried. I'm afraid she is going to send us back. I love living here."

"I know. What can we do? I feel so helpless," she says. "Have you talked with her?"

"No, I keep pretending that if I don't ask, it won't happen." I sigh. "I just can't seem to talk to her. The gap is too wide. I want her to love me, for her to see me for who I am. But how can she when she has no clue and makes no effort to find out? I don't think she can."

"You need to know. You must ask her," Lydia says softly.

Little do I know the die is already cast.

At the bottom of the road, I say goodbye. "See you Friday," we both say at the same time, laughing, which relieves the tension and lets us focus on something we have some control over. Lydia goes back up the hill, and I walk along the promenade toward The Dock—a route I have walked at least several hundred times.

She's right. I need to ask Mother about her intention. Is she sending us back? I need to confront this. What is the worst that can happen? I am already afraid that she is sending us back. I already know she is not capable of connecting with me in the way I had hoped. She has given

me a safe haven—for that, I am grateful—but no emotional connection, and she has abandoned us before. Twice. What's to keep her from
doing it again?

Lost in thought, I suddenly become more aware of my surroundings. The night is damp and cold, and, as predicted, there is
a thick, misty fog billowing in and out over the road, following the
wind, creating odd gray shadows in the mist between the streetlights. Looking forward along the promenade, I see the areas of
illumination around the streetlights appear as havens of soft and
shifting shadows in the overall dark and gloomy spaces between.
Pale yellow lights can be seen from the front-room windows of
the row houses on the other side of the street, signaling occupants
most likely wrapped up in front of the fire watching the telly on a
cold and wet night like this.

I like to walk along the promenade walkway. It is smoother than
the sidewalk across the road with its cracks and ruptures in the cobblestone blocks. The promenade is easier to walk along, less hazard-
ous, especially in the dark. Besides, I like to listen to the sound of the
water as it moves over the pebbles and rocks on the beach, and the
waves lapping and sometimes crashing up on the beach below. It is
one of my favorite walks. *I love the wildness of Cornwall the most*, I
muse.

I can't see the moon or stars. The sky is dark with clouds, obscured
by the murky fog. There is no rain; instead there is a miserable drizzle.
I reach up to draw my coat close and wrap my scarf another round
about my neck to shut out the cold wind seeping in below my collar. I
shiver and realize I don't hear any sound. *The tide must be out.*

I cannot hear the waves crashing against the rocks, which seems
odd since there is a wind. There is a sudden stillness in the air.

*Did I hear a sound? No, it's nothing. Why is everything so silent? It
must be the fog muffling the sounds of the sea, and there is no one else
about to make noise.*

I feel a subtle shift in the air. Suddenly, an electric jolt of energy courses through my body from head to toe, every sense on high alert. I am not sure what the danger is, but I am certain there *is* a danger. I know it! I feel it. My body tenses, getting ready for something, getting prepared to respond to the roaring, unbidden voice ricocheting in my head.

Flee! Run!

The hair on the back of my neck rises, and there is another silent cry. *Don't look back! Flee!*

Poised on the edge of running, I pause. *Keep calm. It's nothing. It's all right. Breathe. It's the fog.* I attempt to reassure myself, knowing something is wrong and my thoughts are a lie.

Walking faster, I try to calm myself. *Get a grip*, I tell myself in a harsher tone.

I take another deep breath, afraid to run, afraid not to run, but my eyes continually search for a safe haven, even though I know there isn't one at this end of the road. I am nearing the beginning of the public sea pool across from the small Jubilee Garden and the alley that leads to the back entrance of The Dock. This is the most isolated part of the promenade.

Another thought ricochets through my mind. *I won't have time to get there; it's too far.* Increasing my stride again, I move as quickly as I can through the shadows and mists, trying to escape whatever it is that is behind. The surge of energy propels me through the fog that continues to billow in and around the lights—lights that now seem very far apart.

Suddenly, from the corner of my eye, two shapes emerge from the side street at the edge of the garden. As the fog shifts, I see it is Mr. Trenowith and his son, Branok, local fishermen who come for an evening pint at The Dock Hotel.

I break into a full run and shout, "Hey there, Branok! Mr. Trenowith, hold up! I'll walk with you to The Dock."

They both turn at the sound of my voice and stop under the light at the end of the road waiting. "Hello, Diana," Mr. Trenowith says. "What are you doing out in this miserable weather?"

"Returning from a friend's house," I gasp out, trying to catch my breath. I walk as close as I can, glad to see the alley leading to The Dock coming up on our left. We turn down the walkway together, and with a sigh of relief, I see the back door of The Dock just ahead. In seconds, I'm in the back half of the pub.

I am safe. Breathe. I am safe.

I turn to Mr. Trenowith and Branok. "Thank you. I was frightened for a moment in the fog. Thank you for waiting."

Mr. Trenowith tips his cap, nods his head in acknowledgment, and walks down the hall to the pub for his pint. Branok stays back a moment.

"Well, if you need an escort in the future, do let me know," he says with a wink and a smile before he, too, walks down the hall to the pub. Branok often flirts and teases.

I go to my room, but I am afraid to go up into the dark hallway. Instead, I sit out of sight on the landing, hunched against the wall, my arms wrapped around my body. I am cold and shivering; my teeth chatter. I try to process what happened, but I am still gripped by fear and unwilling to go into the empty hotel above.

I will wait until Mother and Stan come up after the pub closes. We sleep upstairs when there are no winter guests.

Sitting on the landing, I feel desolate. My heart pounds, and my breath is short. Never once, in the almost two years I have been in England, have I felt afraid—never—in the hotel, in the town, on the promenade, on long walks in the countryside, in the villages, or on the cliffs, day or night. Not once.

Well, there was one time a creepy guy gave me a ride when I was out. I didn't like it the minute I got inside the car, so I made him pull over to let me out. I walked the rest of the way home. This time the fear came out of nowhere, more shocking for its suddenness and ferocity. I am once again vulnerable. The world, once again, is unsafe.

I must be extraordinarily lucky or extraordinarily stupid—or both. How could I forget to be vigilant? I let my guard down. Foolish! Fool! Have I not learned that I have to be on guard all of the time? I forgot.

I am stunned. My heart sinks. My world, my haven, the bold and beautiful place that I live in, is tarnished. I let my guard down.

I pretended I was safe, and I was not—a vast disappointment. A portent?

22
Strike Three

I've talked myself into thinking my fright Wednesday night was caused by the fog and that I scared myself for no reason.

I don't tell my mother what happened. She might restrict me. I do, however, change my tactics. I won't let this experience prevent me from going out, but I will be more careful. I have warned David to be careful. Jamie doesn't go out after dark.

Lydia and I devise an alternative route to her house. The plan is that if I am out after dark, I will stay at Lydia's. If I am without clothes, I can wear something of Lydia's until I get back home. Instead of returning to The Dock along the waterfront, I will go through town. Lydia and Rosalie will walk me up to the high road until we are among other people. Then they will return back together to their house. I will go to The Dock from the middle of town, waiting to tag along with someone walking down Chapel Street. It is a longer distance, but more people are about. I am glad I still have survival skills and am very aware of how lucky I was that Mr. Trenowith and Branok came along that night. If it should happen again, I might not be so fortunate. I am scared and alert.

After work on Friday, I walk back to The Dock, change clothes, and check on my brother. He is staying in for the night.

"Don't forget about Sunday. I'm taking you and Jamie for fish and chips and a movie."

"OK," he replies.

"And don't forget what I said about going out at night."

Earlier I had warned him that he needs to be alert to what is going on around him when he is out, to be with a group, and to stay in after dark.

The night is, again, wet and miserable. Lydia, Rosalie, and I walk to the Winter Gardens. Halfway down, we agree the weather is too much. Instead, we turn around, go back, and find something else to do.

"I know!" says Rosalie. "We can try the Ouija board we got for Christmas."

"Yes," says Lydia. "That will be fun."

"What is a Ouija board?" I ask.

"It's a game," Rosalie responds. "The spirits from beyond answer your questions. Whoooo!" she laughs.

"Yes, it will be fun. Mysterious and mystifying." Lydia and Rosalie laugh again. "It will be all right," they chorus together.

I don't like the idea. I'm not much for ghosts and spirits of the dead. I have a relationship with death, and I don't like this game. Something very frightening just happened, and I can't explain it. I don't want to open the door for another experience.

However, the Cornish live in a culture and history steeped with magic, good and bad. Bedtime stories include witches and goblins and other creatures of the night. These are not things to be afraid of. Mostly.

Apprehensively, I think, *You didn't experience what was behind me the other night. I'm not sure I want to contact and receive messages from spirits or have anything to do with ghosts or beings from beyond.*

Even so, I reluctantly agree, "OK, OK, it's only a game." I don't want my fears to get in the way, and we will be safe inside the Tellam house.

We arrive back at the house, welcoming the warm fire in the grate. We make a cup of tea and set up the small table in front of the fire for the game.

"Let me see the box," I say to Rosalie. "I want to read about 'mysterious and mystifying' myself." Rosalie hands over the box. "The directions say we should put the board on our laps between us, or we can put it on the table."

I continue reading. "Assemble the game piece." I hold up the planchette and the little "feet" that screw into the bottom to lift the planchette off the board and help it to slide easily across the surface. Once the board has been put together, two of us will sit across from each other, balance the board, and put our fingers on the planchette.

I stop reading for a moment and comment, "That seems simple enough."

Once we are set up, we are supposed to concentrate on our question, asking the spirit world what we want to know, and then hope a spirit is moved to answer the question. "The planchette is supposed to move across the board if the spirits respond," I say as Rosalie readies herself to be the first to ask a question.

She moves over by the fire and sits across from Lydia, balancing the board across their knees. "Does Brian want to be my boyfriend?" she asks in a soft voice, which makes me wonder if she really wants to know the answer to the question.

The planchette, shaped like an upside-down heart with a hole in the middle, starts to slowly move across the board. It is clearly moving to the upper right side of the board, across the arched letters toward the sun and the answer "yes." Rosalie's eyes are open, and her smile is wide as she feels the piece move across the board.

"Whoa!" we all say, surprised that there is a response and that it is so quick.

"I didn't move the planchette," Rosalie assures us.

"Me neither," says Lydia.

I look around the room, wondering about spirits. I don't see anything. I don't feel anything scary, so I relax a little.

Lydia is next. I'm still not anxious to ask a question.

Lydia's question is about her schoolwork. "Will I do well in the exam next week?" she asks. Again, the planchette moves quickly across the board toward "yes."

"Looks positive," I say.

"Yes, but I still have to study," she says with a smile.

Now it is my turn, and I exchange places with Rosalie and put the board across my lap and Lydia's. I am nervous and tense. I don't like the idea of messing with spirits and the occult. I shake off the feeling and put my fingers on the board. The planchette feels smooth beneath my fingers and moves easily on the board. Looking down on the board from above, I am struck by the twenty-six letters arched across the middle of the board in two rows of thirteen letters. I wonder if there is significance to the layout. I can understand the "yes" and "no" options, and the sun and moon on the upper right and left corners, but I'm not sure what the faces on the bottom right and left corners mean.

I haven't decided on a question, but I have been worried as February approaches. It is three weeks until the two-year mark of my arrival in Cornwall. Mother has said nothing about returning us to Calvin, but I remember his parting words. I am hoping my mother will tell him no and let us stay. She has said nothing either way. We are half-British, so she could try. I am ever hopeful, though my optimism is unfounded. I impulsively decide what my question to the Ouija will be.

"I might as well get the suspense over," I say with a laugh when I tell Rosalie and Lydia my decision.

On impulse, I blurt out, "Will I be returning to America?"

We hardly have time to settle our fingers on the planchette and close our eyes to concentrate when the piece starts to move across the board. The movement is so smooth and definite, gliding across the board without hesitation. I open my eyes and see that the planchette, under the guidance of Lydia's and my hands, is moving to the upper corner of the board. Toward the sun and "yes."

I'm going back to America.

"Oh, no!" I say out loud. "I don't want to."

And then, foolishly, without waiting or thinking, our hands still on the planchette, I blurt out another question. "When?" I ask in a soft and disbelieving voice. "When am I going back to America?"

Slowly but surely, the planchette starts to move under our fingers, making its way down the board to the ten numbers across the bottom. The planchette point stops at number three.

Three. Three weeks is the anniversary date of our arrival. I grasp the meaning. *Three weeks. Calvin said two years, no more. The two years are up in three weeks.*

I cry out, "I don't want to go!" and quickly pull my fingers up from the board.

"This is silly," I say, knowing in my heart it is probably true. I am frightened that maybe it is true. My heart is full of dread.

David and I are going back to America. I didn't ask about David, but I presume he is too.

Was it a spirit? I wonder. *Would a spirit lie? Probably not. How would it know?*

"OK, that's enough for me," I say. "No more Ouija; you two go ahead if you want." I move over to sit closer to the fire, as I am suddenly bone cold.

"It's just a game," Lydia says, rushing to console me, putting her arm around my shoulder.

Unfortunately, I don't believe her, but I can't say that. She is my friend.

I'm going home. I am dismayed as I try to absorb the meaning of the message, and my heart rebels with a resounding, *No!* Maybe this time, she will step up and claim us. In my imagination, she tells

Calvin she is not sending us back. *Optimistic on my part. Foolishly, I even hope Calvin might have forgotten.*

Lydia, Rosalie, and I spend the rest of the evening talking about anything but my return to America. None of us wants to go there, least of all me. The Ouija board is dismantled and put away in the closet. We sit by the fire and play gin rummy. When I return to The Dock the next afternoon, I will ask my mother what is going to happen.

The next day, Lydia walks me halfway to The Dock.

"I don't want to go home, Lydia. I want to stay here."

"I know," she replies. "What can we do? I feel so helpless."

"Me too." I dread what is to come if the Ouija board is correct. *I hope it is not true, but where has hope led me in the past? Nowhere.* It is good to have a friend beside me while I process the prospect of returning to America. Confusion threatens to overwhelm me. I am deeply troubled by the thought of going "home." But how can I still think of America as home? Cornwall feels like home. I love living here. Don't I belong here more than in America?

Lydia turns back at the top of the hill while I turn to walk along Main Street before I turn down Chapel Street and head to The Dock. *As soon as I get back to The Dock, that's when I'll approach her.* I prep for the meeting.

Entering the door, I can either go left and into the sitting room, or, because it is winter, I can go upstairs to my small bedroom. I am late, but perhaps it is not too late to talk with her. I go to the family room. But my mother is unusually absent from the premises; she usually comes up to the living room for a few hours in the afternoon/early evening. On Saturday night, she doesn't come up to the family room all evening. She stays in the bar. On Sunday, when I am in, she is out. *Is she avoiding me?* I wonder.

The boys and I go to the movies and for fish and chips on Sunday afternoon and then return home. I am determined to confront my mother at the first possible moment.

My determination is thwarted. My mother stays in the bar on Sunday evening.

I go to work on Monday morning as usual. I'm troubled by what appears to be an effort at avoidance by my mother. We don't interact much, but her absence seems unusual. I am still hopeful that "the spirits" are wrong, and the Ouija board was just a game.

I have an endless capacity to delude myself, to hope for the best—but somehow miss that target, and the worst happens.

The following Monday, I am surprised to see my mother in the living room when I get home from work. As I walk in the door, I glance at my mother, and she avoids eye contact, not greeting me. I can see from the flush on her cheeks that she has been drinking. Her face always gets red when she drinks. My eyes rove around the room, taking it in, and I see what looks like a ticket folder on the dining room table.

"You're sending us back," I blurt out, not waiting for her to speak. "Please don't, not yet."

She ignores my plea and continues to avoid meeting my eyes, her body shifting in the chair. Her blue dress is stretched across her ample hips, her feet crossed and tucked under the chair.

Finally, she looks up. "Stanley and I can't keep you here any longer. Your father is demanding your return home. These just arrived in the mail today." She is implying the tickets came from my father, although she was to pay for our return—that was part of the agreement my father had with my mother. I know she is lying.

"Your father expects you back in two weeks. I have to send you back."

"Please don't, not yet. Did you talk to him?" I ask.

"Yes, we talked on the phone. He says to send you back," she replies, and then repeats herself: "Stanley and I have discussed this, and we cannot keep you here."

I take a minute to process the words. I suspect the first part is more truthful than the last part. This is an old story. It is a story I heard when my mother betrayed us the first time. My father says she didn't want us or only wanted two of us. She says my father wouldn't let her have us. He might have said, "All or nothing." He got the all.

I believed the story for a while, but not since the second betrayal when she sent us back to my father's house from Switzerland. She knew what she was sending us back to, and she did it anyway.

Just as she is making a choice to send us back this time.

I'm not so gullible anymore. I listen to tone and cadence as well as words, and I know my mother is not being honest.

"Stanley and I can't keep you."

That means she doesn't want to, probably at his urging. She doesn't take responsibility for her actions; it is always somebody else who is at fault or prevents her from doing something . . . doing the right thing.

Stanley didn't want us when she left us the first time. It is clear Stanley didn't want us these past two years. This is old news.

"You talked to Calvin?" I ask again.

"Yes, we talked a few weeks ago. Calvin said to send you home," she says in a false voice, still not looking up.

Weeks ago?

"I don't want to go back to America," I cry out again. "You could keep us if you want to. I'll pay more rent. I'll get a second job and pay for David." I can hear the pleading in my voice. "I don't mind."

"No," she says again. "Stanley and I can't keep you."

In other words, she doesn't want to.

She is not owning that she controls the money and makes choices in her relationship with Stanley. She has a private income and is from a wealthy family. She could provide for us. She is not owning that there is little that Calvin is likely to do if she just says no. He wouldn't get on a plane and come to England to claim us—he doesn't have the money. She blames her betrayal on Calvin each time. She fails to see the irony that by her choices, she leaves us, the victims, to a man she was not willing to live with. For her own benefit, not ours, she left us the first time. She sent us back again from Switzerland. Now she is sending us back again.

She hunches over and away from me. I can see the inevitability of return in the set of her shoulders. She positions herself so she doesn't have to look at me. She is unwilling to face her own deceit—end of story. The proof is in the plane tickets on the table: flights scheduled for exactly two years from the date of arrival. Strike three.

Section 6:
The Path to Emancipation

23

Leaving England

I am restless in the night, thoughts tumbling through my mind like whirlwinds, ricocheting mostly disappointment and anger with my mother.

She's done it again.

Repetitive thoughts reel through my mind as my mother's actions intrude on my efforts to think through what it means to return to my father's house. Thumping my pillow in despair, I find it hard to contain my sense of outrage at my mother's betrayal once again and my utter lack of control over my own life.

Stuff it in the Well, Diana, and move on.

Reverting to old ways of managing, I focus on practical things. *What do I have to do to prepare for the return?*

I've had no word from Calvin in two years. I have no idea what we are going back to. *Probably more of the same. Is Calvin still married to Dorothy? Are Dorothy's children still living with them? Does he still live in the same farmhouse?*

I don't even know where he lives. The tickets say London to San Francisco—hardly clarifying.

I need to help David pack. I must give notice at my job and ask Mrs. Penwith for a reference. I have to say goodbye to my friends. My thoughts scatter across a myriad of things that must be done. *Ten days is not long enough to prepare. How do I say goodbye to this place?*

We are flying into the unknown and familiar uncertainty.

Miscellaneous tasks form a list in my mind, things that must be done. I will deal with grief later.

Then my heart speaks. *I want time to roam again in the hedges and across the headlands, walk on the cliffs, and watch the waves roar in on the winter tides.*

I must absorb as much of the sights and sounds of this place as I can, imprinting memories within my mind and heart, memories that can be resurrected later, when I want, when I need to remember.

I have been happy in this place.

Whatever happened in the fog a few nights ago scared me. Terrifying as it happened, it left me with remnants of fear that I have to contend with. I won't walk alone along the promenade at night. But I can't let the fear stop me from making the most of my last few days in Cornwall.

A sigh escapes.

I had hoped I would find a connection with my mother, some kind of interaction beyond the surface, something real, perhaps even that she loved me or that I loved her.

I don't know why she brought us here, what she hoped for.

Whatever it was, it didn't happen. Or maybe it did.

I have no idea. Still, I am grateful she brought us to Cornwall to live a life away from Calvin.

She took steps to fix my teeth, provided me with stylish if conservative clothes, and exposed me to countless new experiences. She brought me to Cornwall and the sea. I gained confidence, worked, earned a living, saved money, and made friends. I connected with the world outside myself and the world within.

I am grateful for the time to become who I am, without significant restriction. I am not the same frightened, anxious, fearful child I was two years earlier. It is a hard lesson to accept that my mother is not able to love me in a way that I need or understand. It is a hard lesson to acknowledge her for who she is, rather than what I want her to be. I know I can't depend on her.

I will be leaving England a changed person.

These two years have been an immeasurable gift—even if she doesn't understand what she has bestowed.

As I walk to work on Tuesday morning, I think about telling Mrs. Penwith that I am leaving. When I enter the office, she lifts her cheery face and greets me.

"Good morning, Diana. There is a pot of fresh tea on the sideboard. It is cold out this morning. Come and warm yourself by the grate."

"Yes, it is cold," I reply as I walk over to the sideboard to pour a cup of tea, adding a touch of sugar to sweeten it. I stand near the grate to get warm.

No sense in waiting.

"Mrs. Penwith, I have bad news. I'm very sorry, but I must give notice at the end of the week. I am returning to America next week." I take a deep breath. "I need to work out resignation with you and would like to ask if you would provide me with a letter of reference so I can try to work in America."

"Oh, Diana, I'm sorry to hear that! I know you want to stay."

I don't have more to say at this point. I am angry, but not at Mrs. Penwith.

"I'm sorry to inconvenience you with such short notice."

"Not a problem, dear. My niece is coming to visit for a few weeks, and she can step in and help until I find someone else. If you can finish up last month's books by the end of the week, I can manage the rest."

"Thank you. That will give me a few days to say a proper farewell to Cornwall."

"Aye, you do that. I'll have your reference letter ready by the end of work tomorrow."

Mrs. Penwith returns to her work, and I go to my desk to begin entering orders into the ledger, my first task of the day. After work, I can focus on packing and planning the rest of my time in Cornwall.

Friday night will be my last time at the Winter Gardens. Lydia and I plan to go so I can say goodbye to my other friends. I'll stay over at the Tellams' as usual.

When we arrive at the Winter Gardens, I plan to say a quiet goodbye, soak up the memories and relish this last time with my friends. That's before Lydia steps in and announces on the microphone that I will be leaving, and that everyone should stop by, have a dance, and say goodbye.

"Sorry to hear you are leaving," Richard says.

"You're not a bad sort for an American," Gordon says with a smile in his eyes. "Sorry to see you go."

"Come back again soon," Mary and Jenny say in unison. "It's been lovely to get to know you."

The well-wishes and dances continue throughout the evening, with old and new friends. It is a fun night, and I am grateful for the good wishes from the many people I have met on our Friday nights at the Winter Gardens. It is a fond memory to take with me.

Lydia and her family are away the following weekend, so we plan on tea the following Wednesday to say my final farewells. I want to thank them for including me in their family. My friendship with Lydia has been one of the highlights of my time in Cornwall. She is my first friend, and I am grateful for that friendship, grateful to know what it feels like to have a friend. She taught me the joy of sharing my thoughts and feelings with someone who shared with me too. She was someone to have fun and go on adventures with. It was a friendship that allowed me to be myself, a fifteen-year-old girl, an adolescent. I felt less lonely here with Lydia as my friend. I will miss her.

The future seems bleak, as if I am going backward, not forward. I dread the possibility of returning to isolation and the toxic atmosphere of my father's house.

On Saturday morning, I take the bus to Sennen Cove and Porthcurno. I take in the fields, hedgerows, and narrow lanes leading to the villages at the edge of the sea. The bus meanders along the coast, stopping occasionally along the way. I am anxious to get outside onto the headland.

I want to feel the cold bite of the wind on my face, feel the wind ruffle my hair, see the gulls swooping down, looking for their dinner in the waters off the headland. I want to walk through the hedgerows, listening to the wind whistle and moan as it travels through the branches and around the bend. I want to savor one last time the smell of the brine and the sound of the sea crashing against the shore and the rocks along the coast. The agitation of the sea will be a perfect complement to the sorrow in my heart.

At Porthcurno, I climb the cliffs and find a place to shelter among the granite boulders as I watch and listen to the waves crashing against the massive cliffs. The turbulence of the sea matches my emotion—the anger I feel at my mother's betrayal.

I can't do this. I can't go back. But I know I have no choice. I can't take care of David on my own, and I can't let him go back alone. *I have to go.*

I take solace in the sea and the wind a while longer. I climb the cliff to the road to catch the bus back to Penzance. Glancing around, I say my farewell.

The rest of the week is a blur. I have to close out my bank account and the health insurance stamps. I need to change my English money into American dollars. I have nothing to say to my mother or Stanley. I say a fond farewell to the regulars in the pub and others who have been part of my life in Cornwall. It is a bittersweet farewell on Wednesday night as I join the Tellams for tea.

Mrs. Tellam wishes me well. "It's been a pleasure knowing you, Diana. Thank you for being a good friend to my girls."

Rosalie tries to be upbeat. "Things will be different now," she says, giving my shoulder a squeeze as she walks behind me to get more water for the tea. "You're older now. Perhaps it won't be so bad."

Ha! I know there is little use in telling Rosalie she has no idea what life in America was like or will be like.

"I'll miss your friendship," Lydia says, tears pooling in the corners of her eyes. "I wish you didn't have to leave."

"Me too, Lydia. I can't bear to leave, but I must. Thank you for being my friend."

Lydia and Rosalie walk me up to the top of the road as I give them a last hug goodbye. I turn down the lane to The Dock, my final hours in Cornwall at hand.

My mother, David, and I travel again on the night train, this time back to London. I'm glad it is the night train—less time I have to spend sitting across from my mother in the confined space of the train compartment she has rented. Upon boarding the train, David and I go to the restaurant car for dinner. My mother stops at the bar for a drink.

Good. The bitterness would gag me if I had to sit across from my mother and pretend everything is all right.

David and I sleep through the night, lulled to sleep by the sound of the train wheels rolling along the track. At breakfast, we go again to the restaurant car, while my mother continues to sleep. I take this opportunity to talk with my brother.

"David, I don't know what it will be like when we get back to California. I'll do the best I can to protect you."

"That's all right, sis. I know you will. What will be, will be. I'm bigger now too."

How did David get so smart for someone so young?

"We can talk more on the plane. It will be a long flight," I reply, as we return to the compartment to collect our belongings. The train is slowing as we enter Paddington Station. My mother is waiting for us.

"We'll catch a cab to the airport," she says, as we collect our belongings.

"Fine."

We ride in silence across London to Heathrow Airport.

My mother has arranged for someone from the airline to meet us at the ticket counter and take us through customs and to the plane, so she can return on the next train to Penzance. She offers a lame excuse.

"I have to be back at the pub to work tonight."

Right! She runs the place; she can decide if she has to work or not.

I wonder if she accompanied us because she thought we might run away. I wish I *could* run away.

"There is an airline assistant." My mother points to a tall woman standing on the left of the Continental Airlines sign. Her job done, she says abruptly, "Right then. I'll be off."

I walk toward the person my mother has pointed to. I have nothing to say to my mother. I don't wait to see what David does; that is between him and my mother. There is no way I am going to make her betrayal easy for her. Our flight leaves in two hours. She couldn't even wait to see us through the gate.

Once we board, David and I settle in. It is an eleven-hour flight to San Francisco. I say to David, "I'll stay as long as I can to look after you."

"Don't worry, I'll be fine."

While David watches the movie, I think about the past two years in Cornwall. It has been hard at my mother's in many ways. She is incapable of giving me the love that I want from her, she tolerated Stanley's assault on my self-esteem, and she was generally negligent. However, I am also immensely grateful to her for enabling my freedom and giving me time to learn who I am, to make friends, to have fun. It has confirmed that life can be different from the experience I had known with Calvin.

It has given me hope and a goal. It is an immeasurable gift—even if she didn't realize she bestowed it. I have changed from a quiet, invisible child to a full-blown, semi-confident teenager. For the past year, I have worked, lived independently, bought my clothes and food, made friends, survived disappointments, had adventures. I have savings in my pocket. I am sixteen, and I know I will manage if I can find a way out.

Random thoughts float through my mind as I look down on the clouds outside the window as we fly back to life with my father.

I'm not going back to live a life of fear. I'll have to speak up and tell him we are not the same children who left two years ago . . . Yeah, right!

I lean against the window and watch the sun begin to set on the edge of the horizon. I wonder how my father will handle two teenagers who know there is a better way to live.

24

Return to America

The plane descends, and the earth rises up to meet the wheels.
Here we go. Who knows what is in store for us?

The deceleration causes me to jerk back in the seat as the plane touches down on the ground. Not a smooth landing. Likely a forewarning of things to come.

David and I are back in America—a place I do not want to be. I have tasted freedom. This newfound sense of self will likely be a problem in Calvin's household. I have confidence and believe in myself. I have worked; I have lived independently, away from my mother. I bought my own clothes and food and made my own friends. I have been happy.

I say to David, "Are you ready? Remember to keep your head down until we see what the situation is."

I don't know what to expect, so I can't assess a course of action. For now I must live in the grip of uncertainty.

Could there possibly be a fourth stepmother? Oh, please, no!

What I do know is that I am not going to give up on the girl I discovered, the girl who was born and emerged in England. I am not going to cower, be afraid, or be invisible. I sound brave in my head, but I don't exactly have plans to stand up to my father either.

I know there will likely be some bumps in the road. I am more afraid of staying with my father than of living independently, but I can't leave David yet. We exit the plane, and David and I process through customs with our two suitcases, full of the remnants of our life in Cornwall. I wonder what my father will look like. The old feelings of tension and vigilance in my father's orbit resurface as we move closer to his physical presence. *We'll know soon enough.*

The customs agent stamps our passports for entry back into the United States. I am stiff, my spine straight as we go through the last exit door. I see my father instantly, alone, readily recognizable in the distance on the edge of the crowd outside the big green exit doors. He is standing tall, his shock of gunmetal-gray hair distinct among the people who are waiting. He is a big man, but not as big as he once seemed. I am taller now, but not tall enough; he still towers over me. With eyes gaunt and hooded, his leathery, tanned face looks stern and unforgiving. Little has changed. He is as I remember him.

Walking toward him, I take in the details. His shirtsleeves are rolled up, and one arm is browner than the other. He leans his left arm on the window ledge as he drives, so it is always browner than the other arm. I see by his stance that he is taking our measure as we walk toward him. He is dressed in a white shirt and pants, the ever-present black belt cinched around his middle. These are his work clothes; he must have come from his cook's job at the nearby prison.

"Come on, David. Calvin is over there."

As we near Calvin, he speaks gruffly, "Are these all of your bags?"

"Yes, this is everything."

There is no greeting, no hug, no warm smile, no "welcome home." He simply lifts his index finger and points in the direction of the parking lot. As we walk behind him across the street, I look over to David and say, "Here we go."

I see the station wagon ahead on the right, the car he drove before we left.

That hasn't changed either.

We load our luggage into the back, and I get in the middle seat, sitting behind my father, who is in the driver's seat. I am alert, my back straight, my hands in my lap. David sits next to me, on the right, behind the passenger seat. When I glance over at David to check on him, he seems relaxed.

Maybe he is tired. Perhaps he can handle this better than I can. He is still young.

My father heads south. We are going toward Sacramento. My heart cries out in protest. I can only assume that my father's current living situation is the same as when we left two years ago. Mostly, I look out the window, staring at the winter hills as we leave San Francisco, drive through Vallejo, and descend into the Sacramento Valley. I pat David on the arm reassuringly, although I don't say anything. David and I have talked about what it will be like to be back, and we both have an idea what to expect.

I haven't decided yet what to say or when to say it to my father. I do not have a particular strategy. I want to speak out, but I am afraid. I continue to stare at the rolling hills as we speed down the road, my thoughts rambling on.

I am not going to give up on the girl I discovered, the girl who was born in England. I am not going to cower, be afraid, be invisible. I feel a strange sense of peace. I am not exactly going to stand up to my father either, except maybe just once.

I glance up in the car and see that my father is watching me in the rearview mirror. At first, I look away, watching the scenery slide by as we drive down over the Vallejo Hills into the valley. It is still winter, and the hills are green; they will be golden brown by summer.

I look back again, and he is still watching me. Quaking inside, I hold his gaze, taking his measure as he takes mine. I have not planned this moment, not intended to confront him yet, but it seems right; it feels like the time.

This is it. This is when I must take my stand. Calvin will have to pull over to hit me, and that might give me time to prepare. It is now or never.

I look him in the eye in the mirror, and after a moment, I take a deep breath and slowly, deliberately open my mouth, waiting for words to come out.

I hold his gaze as the words tumble out. "If you ever hit David or me again, I will never speak to you for the rest of your life." My voice is slow, calm, clear, and determined. A shiver runs down my back when I realize what I have done. I break the gaze.

OMG, what did I just do? Am I crazy? What does he care whether I talk to him or not? What have I unleashed by my impulsive behavior?

But there is silence in return, no words, no yelling, no loss of temper. He does not pull the car over or reach back to punch me. He does not say anything. He just looks at me in the mirror for a few more moments, then he, too, looks away. Though he doesn't say anything, I know he heard me. I said it loud enough. His silence leaves me to ponder what is next. Perhaps he can see that I am no longer a child.

Maybe I reminded him of himself or my mother—who knows? I never knew what my father was thinking. I never understood why he did what he did. He was an unknown to me.

David looks over at me and mouths, "Way to go, sis!" He smiles in admiration.

I watch as my father changes lanes, moving the car over to the right lane on the freeway. The exit he takes means it is likely that he lives in the same house we lived in when we left, an old farmhouse outside of town. The area is mostly flat agricultural land northeast of Sacramento, famous for almond groves that spread out over the landscape and for the prison on the edge of town. There used to be more cattle ranches, hence the town's name, Vacaville. We are going to live again in the country outside of "cow town."

My "victory" doesn't mean I'm safe. This small challenge does not mean life is free of fear. I am vigilant. In Calvin's house, vigilance is always warranted; one never knows when something will set him off. One never knows if whatever is in his hand at the moment will go flying toward the offender or offense. One time it was a hammer that sailed across the room, the claw end sticking into the fiberboard wall by the window, narrowly missing my head. He throws things in anger, on impulse, not considering if anyone will be hurt by his action. I have to remind David again to be vigilant.

Surprisingly, my words to my father seem to change the status, the atmosphere between him and me. He doesn't seem as menacing and unpredictable as he used to be. He doesn't talk to me. He doesn't single me out. He is just a presence. Time will tell if anything is really different.

In the meantime, I resume my old strategy of fading into the background, of vigilance as I work toward independence. I will look after David.

25

Moving Toward Freedom

I am in America, in California. It is a huge blow, a disappointment. I will have to rise to the occasion—survive and emancipate.

Though I don't know it yet, I have returned in 1966 to a changed and changing America. California is an epicenter of generational change—change that germinates as I grow into my own transformation. A metamorphosis and a changing environment make for an exciting combination as I navigate the changes in my life. I almost feel optimistic.

I must survive my father's household until David is old enough for me to leave.

We turn down the road, and I see the farmhouse ahead. As we enter into the driveway, Becky and John come out the back door and around to the car. Becky has a big grin on her face.

Dorothy appears at the back door as we unload the suitcases and yells, "Y'all come in for something to eat. It's late, but you must be hungry. I've saved some food for you."

She made food for us. She didn't hurt us before. This might be survivable.

I stop and look around for a minute. The yard is the same, a big oak tree in the front with a tire swing. Mostly empty fields are barren before the spring planting. Odd houses dot the horizon. The night sky is a leaded gray, no rain but cold and icy.

The house is the same: a one-story, unpainted wood farmhouse from the 1920s or 1930s with a front porch and a back stoop. We enter through the kitchen, filing in one after another. It, too, looks the same: drab brown linoleum on the floor, a yellow Formica table near the kitchen sink, chairs with yellow plastic seats and metal frames, and a metal sink and a long shelf along the wall. The table serves as a countertop/chopping/food preparation area. There is a wooden dining table in an alcove. The living room is also drab, with a brown couch at one end and a television at the other. Off the living room is the bedroom I will share with Becky, and in the middle is the room David will share with John. Calvin and Dorothy's bedroom is on the other side of the living room.

Becky smiles, while John stands silent in the corner. He is big and beefy like his mother. Becky seems much the same as I remember her: a big smile and a sparkle in her eye. She reminds me that the room we share together is on the left, as we go into the living room. We enter the small bedroom with two single beds and a window with a white window curtain, a small closet off to the side.

"Remember, the bed on the right is yours." Becky points to the bed against the inside wall. "I have to clean the dishes now," she says over her shoulder as she leaves the room. She doesn't seem resentful at having to share the room; a smile came readily to her face.

At dinner, my father, David, and I sit silently as we eat. It's been a while since I have eaten grits and beans. I had forgotten about southern food. When my father is finished, he sets down his fork, looks up, and tells us of our future.

"You can rest tomorrow, then you will be assigned chores. You will attend church. Dorothy will take you to enroll in school on Monday. I have to work."

Good news. We are going to school.

I'd prefer to work and make money than go to school because I already know that money is the key to freedom. If going to school will help me get more money and a better job, then I'll do it. Money means independence. I don't need a lot of money, just enough for food, rent, and transportation. I will need to be able to support David too. My brother John still lives in Southern California, and Patsy and her family are in Sacramento. I don't know when we will get to see them.

On Monday morning, Dorothy drives David and me to the local high school and takes us into the school office. It is not clear what grades we will be in. David went to school in England for two years, but I did not. The school counselor advises Dorothy that we have to take tests to determine our academic skill level, then we will be assigned grades.

Dorothy signs some papers and says to us, "Ya'll catch the school bus home. They'll tell you what number." She leaves us in the school office.

After the test results are in, the school counselor advises that David will receive credit for his schooling in England and enter into the last semester of his ninth grade. He is delighted by this outcome. My situation is more complicated. While I sit in the school counselor's office, I see some pamphlets with information about school credit for work experience. I might be eligible for a work experience program that allows educational credit for work I did while in England. This is a promising possibility.

When it is my turn to talk with the counselor, I walk into his office and he gives me a friendly greeting.

"Hi, Ms. English. I'm Mr. Burns. Glad to meet you. I'm your school counselor and will help figure out what to do about your education."

"Hi, I'm Diana. I noticed the pamphlet about work experience. I'd be happy to talk with you about my work experience while I was in England. I worked in a hotel, a restaurant, a hospital nursing program, and as a clerk in a general store."

I pull out the recommendation letter from Mrs. Penwith and hand it to Mr. Burns.

"This looks very impressive," he says. "But there is an issue of meeting graduation requirements. We can give you credit for your work experience, but you must take social studies, English, and a math class."

I learn I will need to attend school for two semesters to meet the necessary graduation requirements. If I finish the February–June term, and then September–December, I can graduate in January. In less than a year, I can be free. I can also take classes like typing and accounting that will help me get a better job. Right now, my work options are babysitting or working in a fast-food place.

Less than a year. I can do this. I sigh in relief.

Life settles into a routine: school during the week and church on Sunday morning, Sunday evening, and Wednesday evening. Calvin seems subdued. While there is tension in the house, it isn't violent, at least not yet. My father isn't hitting anyone. While I don't have a lot of interaction with Dorothy, she is not mean or hostile. There is food; we keep the house clean. I stay out of the way in my room, do my chores, go to church, and go to school. As soon as the weather improves, life outside in the yard will begin.

Mrs. Brown, the office secretary at the high school, lives down the road from the farmhouse and offers me a job cleaning her house on Saturdays. If I need to stay after school for an activity, she gives me a ride home because she works until 5:00 p.m. I am out of the house most of the time, and when at the house, I do my chores, study, read, watch TV, and keep an eye on David. Somehow the atmosphere does not seem as charged as it was in the past. Violent outbursts from my father still occur unpredictably, but it doesn't feel as tense as it used to. Hopefully, that is not because I have let my defenses down while I was in England. Overall, life seems constricted, but manageable. Mostly.

26

Settling In and Getting Out

I have forgotten that Dorothy is evangelical Pentecostal, a "Holy Roller," which means speaking in tongues and laying on of hands. Serious stuff.

Religion was not a large part of my father's household before Dorothy. It wasn't part of my life in Cornwall, other than what I learned about ancient religions.

Now, however, religion is a central factor.

Rounding out my education, I guess.

Grandmother Maude had been a member of the Church of Christ, and she and Grimes went to church on Sunday. I knew firsthand how hypocritical that was.

May, the Irish girl who was once my "stepmother," and her family were Catholic but not involved in their religion in the way we are now at my father's house. Being a Catholic didn't stop the mean Irish boy.

Perhaps it is just that the Pentecostal religion is more boisterous. I love the hand-slapping, body-moving rhythm of the church music. Becky sings like an angel. She often sings a solo as part of the service. I am not too shocked by the speaking in tongues and hands-on healing.

I read much of the Bible, especially the New Testament, before we went to England. I loved to read. I knew about these kinds of things from evangelical services we attended before we went to England. I think the idea of the Ten Commandments as a way of living is a good blueprint. I'm having a little trouble with the

"honoring thy mother and father" part, but the rest of the commandments seem like sound principles to live by—even if those
around me don't necessarily do so. I want forgiveness for my sins,
which are probably many, and I decide to be baptized. I don't feel
out of step with the teachings, and it is safer at the church than at
home. It is the hypocrisy I can't stand.

I do wonder, though. What is this obsession with sex? Or am I
just more attuned to it because of my earlier experiences? Why, at
least in my experience, are predators attracted to religious institu-
tions or profess their Christianity? Grimes went to church, and so
did my grandmother. They both betrayed me. Children are supposed
to honor their parents. Parents/adults are not admonished to honor
their children? To protect them? To nurture them? Well, parents are
admonished to "spare the rod and spoil the child," a philosophy my
father clearly embraced.

Now, in addition to adolescent boys at church trying to get into
my knickers, an elderly church deacon appears to be weird. Soon
after our return, the family receives an invitation to lunch at the
deacon's home one Sunday after church. He and his wife live in a
distinctive, pink stucco house on the main road, heading out of town.
Perhaps some second sense has developed, but I do not like this man.
I'm wary and watchful. There is something about him that reminds
me of Grimes.

We are not at the house very long when I see him trying to entice
Becky into the back bedroom for some "candy." I step right in.

"Becky, can you come here a minute? I want to ask you about this
song." She joins me in the living room and remains there for the rest
of the visit.

Later, I tell her not to come to this house again.

"Why?" she asks.

"Just trust me," I respond. I explain that we still have to see the
deacon at church, but she needs to stay away from him. Now I wonder

how many victims he might have succeeded in enticing to his bedroom, and if his wife was complicit?

Then there is Dorothy, and whatever issues are going on between her and my father. She and I have an unspoken agreement: she leaves me alone, and I do what she asks me to do and stay out of the way. That's easy enough. These things go together in my experience.

Whenever possible, I read in my room or sit at the end of the couch to watch a TV program in the living room. I do my share of dishes and sweeping the floors. I'm friendly with Becky, but we don't do a lot together unless related to church activities. David behaves about the same, except he is outside more than I am and has outside chores. He is growing tall. He will be as tall as my father when grown, but he has a gentle nature.

One of my last memories of Dorothy is particularly memorable. I am in the living room on the couch reading when Dorothy comes out of her bedroom. I hear her feet thumping on the floorboards and glance up. She is naked and seems intent on crossing the living room to the door between the living room and kitchen where my father is sitting. She does not pay any attention to me. As she stomps across the floor, she raises her very ample stomach, a fleshy ledge on which her breasts sit. Continuing to hold up her stomach with one hand, she reaches down with her other hand to expose her vagina, yelling at my father as she does so.

"Here, old man, look at this! Can't get it up, can you? This is not what I signed up for." When he doesn't respond, she whirls around and returns across the living room to her bedroom. I am stunned. What if David had been in the room?

This is not what I signed up for either. I just have to get through the summer, then school will start again. But even if I escape, what will happen to David?

Later, David and I walk outside to the yard. "How are you getting on, David?"

"Good enough! It's OK if you don't want to live here anymore. I understand. I can take care of myself. I'm almost as big as he is."

"David, do not get into a physical fight with Calvin," I tell him. "He loses control and will not stop until his anger runs out, which can be a long time. Just stay out of his way as much as possible." I pause. "We don't know what will happen—you know how Calvin is. We can make a plan. I only have seven months until I get my diploma. I can get a job to support us."

I am worried about David, but he seems OK.

My prayers are answered. A young family at church needs help with babysitting. The Johnsons, who both work during the day, have two children, ages five and six. They need help with after-school babysitting and in the summer when school is out. The Johnsons live in a duplex in an older neighborhood within walking distance of the high school. Mr. Johnson approaches my father and asks him whether it would be possible for me to help out with babysitting in the afternoons until they get home from work. I can walk the children home and then babysit for a couple of hours. Mrs. Johnson arrives home at 4:45 p.m., and I can walk back to the school and get a ride home from Mrs. Brown, the school secretary.

At the start of summer, Tina (Mrs. Johnson) suggests that I live with them for the summer and babysit during the day while they are at work. I can sleep on a cot at the back of the garage, with a sheet pegged to the ceiling for privacy. I have to come into the house to use the bathroom and eat with the family. Ironing clothes is added to the list of tasks that I am required to do to pay for my keep. The Johnsons are buying my food.

I will earn less and save less, but it is a fair trade-off from my perspective. My father agrees with one requirement. I must continue to attend church, which the Johnsons do regularly, so this is not a problem. I can check on David at church on Sundays and Wednesdays, and he knows how to reach me at the Johnsons'.

This plan works out well: I'm away from home, can still monitor David, and I'm earning money. However, one Sunday in late summer at church, my father announces he is moving the family to Kentucky. He is in some kind of trouble at work and needs to leave town. I am devastated. I don't want to go to Kentucky.

I was there once before we went to England, and I didn't like it at all.

I can't do this! What will I do? What about David?

On Monday, after Tina comes home from work, I tell her about my father's plans.

"I'll talk to Roy and see what he thinks," she says. "Maybe you could stay here with us until you graduate. You would still have to babysit this summer and babysit after school until you graduate."

I sigh with relief. This sounds like an option, especially since I have recently learned that in California, I can be an "emancipated minor" at age sixteen, which means I can get a driver's license, rent an apartment, and have a bank account. It depends on how David feels about being on his own.

"That would be great!" I tell Tina. "I'd like to do that, but I have to talk to David first."

On Sunday, at church, I take David aside. Before I can ask him what he thinks, he says, "I'm OK. I can manage—you don't have to go to Kentucky. I don't blame you. I wouldn't go either, if I could stay. It won't be long before I can leave too."

It is settled. Although I am worried about David, I will stay with the Johnsons to finish school. Once I am independent, I will have David come to live with me.

David leaves for Kentucky with Calvin, Dorothy, Becky, and John. I stay at the Johnsons' and am free to come and go as I want as long as I meet my obligations and the conditions we agreed upon. I babysit the kids from 3:30 to 5:00 p.m. each day after school and sleep in the garage, which is cold in the winter months. I hate the creepy-crawly potato bugs that move across the garage floor at night. I have to be careful before I put my feet on the ground and have to slap my shoes against the floor before I put them on to make sure there are no bugs in them.

I don't make friends easily. I feel out of sync with my fellow students. I have been out of school for two years with vastly different experiences from theirs.

Then suddenly, there is a huge boost in my popularity with the other girls—my brother John comes to visit.

Leaving school one afternoon, I notice this tall, handsome young man sitting on the back of a blue sports car on the circular drive outside the school's main doors. I hear the whispers as the girls congregate outside, waiting for their buses or saying goodbye to their friends at the end of the day.

"Who's that?" they say to each other. "Isn't he cute!"

I look over at the car and realize it is John. I haven't seen him in maybe five years.

"Well, hello, Diana." He motions me over. "Come give your older brother a hug. How are you?"

"Oh my gosh, John! What are you doing here? This is a surprise! Great to see you!"

"I'll give you a ride home. Hop in."

I hop in, and he takes a turn around the driveway, fully aware that everyone on the walkway is staring. This is thrilling to be in a sports car with my handsome brother.

For days afterward, girls come up to me in the hall to ask about my brother. Unfortunately, his visit lasts only a few days, but it is good to see him.

I make a friend in English class, Judy, and hang out with her and her friends sometimes. Mostly, Judy and "the gang" go roller-skating on Friday nights.

I buy a 1950 Ford Coupe and have to learn how to drive a stick shift. That's not the problem; it's the brakes that are not good. Still, the car cost me fifty dollars; I have enough for insurance, and gas is twenty-five cents a gallon. Judy or one of her friends usually picks me up to go to the roller-skating rink in the next town over, so I don't drive that much, anyway. I just want the freedom of having a car.

I smoke cigarettes, something I started in England but couldn't do in front of my father. I also make another friend, Annette. She is new at the school, like I am. Her father is a colonel, stationed at the air force base in the next town over. She is a lot more rebellious than my roller-skating friends.

Annette is sixteen like me. Annette's military family moves often. She is also a wild child, embracing the '60s before I do and dead-locked in battle with her father over everything. A motivated wild child, I am more temperate and go along. In my newfound freedom, Annette and I cut class often to go to the lake on sunny days. Or we go to the bowling alley on the nearby military base, where she is strictly forbidden to go by her father. I am free of my father's rule; she is not. She is a friend and an ally when we both need one.

While in high school, we cut school and do things we are not supposed to. She drives a green-and-white Ford Fairlane, a gift from her father . . . a gift with restrictions. We drive to lots of places on her father's "restricted" list: Lake Berryessa, the military base in Fairfield, and K Street in Sacramento. Early on, she gives me a ride home if I miss the bus.

Before he left, Calvin met Annette and likes that her father is military—but what he likes doesn't matter now because he has already allowed me to emancipate.

Annette has already run away from home several times. I am focused on independence.

Despite cutting school and doing things I shouldn't, I intend to finish high school. I am thinking about next steps and community college. I think I want to be a teacher. I will be graduating in a month, and I am ready for independence. I have saved some money, and I am sure I can get a better job now that I have transportation. I just have to find a place to live.

27

Freedom Isn't All It's Cracked Up to Be, But I'll Take It

I am seventeen, and it is the spring of 1967. I have graduated from high school and moved out of the Johnsons' garage. Multiple field mice and I live in a small duplex on a country road about five miles from town. I can't kill them with mouse traps, and I didn't think to get a cat. I would prefer not to have coresidents, but it is my place. I can afford the rent; I'm independent. If I make bad choices, they are my choices. I am no longer sleeping on a cot at the back of a garage. I have a key, and my apartment is furnished. There is a ratty but clean couch that slouches down in the middle, a small Formica table, two chairs, a basic kitchen, and a bedroom. It is heaven; it is mine. I am an emancipated minor.

I trade my 1950 Ford with no brakes for a black-and-white 1956 Ford convertible with good brakes. I have a car that runs, and when the weather warms up, I can put the top down and ride in the wind. I have a job flipping hamburgers at a roadside stand along the highway working the swing shift. Flipping burgers is a stopgap opportunity. Part of my job is doing the "closing." I don't like working late into the night, but it's busy; it keeps me out of trouble, and the work is not hard. I have a roof over my head and a job to pay for my food, gas, and insurance. I am doing well—at least good enough for the moment while I figure out the next steps.

Although she, too, has graduated from high school, my friend Annette is still living at home.

"Let's move to Sacramento," Annette says. She wants to move away from her father.

"OK, there are probably more jobs there; I will search for a job," I reply. "Let's go look this weekend." I have an advantage because I have work experience.

On Saturday, we drive to Sacramento in my black-and-white '56 Ford convertible. We ride with the top down, enjoying the wind and the sense of freedom. I am buoyed by emancipation and having my own transportation. It is a cool car, especially for dragging K Street in Sacramento on a Friday night, and it's definitely an upgrade from the '50 Ford that was deficient in the brake department.

"Here is an apartment for a hundred fifty dollars per month," Annette says, reading from the For Rent section in the *Sacramento Bee.*

"We have to go cheaper than that. I don't have much money," I sigh. "We can always move up later."

"OK, here is one. Seventy dollars per month," she reads. "It is right downtown, on the main drag."

"Let's look at it," I say.

"No furniture," she replies.

"That's OK. We can manage. Let's look."

The apartment, on the second floor of a commercial building, has one bedroom, a living room, kitchen, and bathroom. There is no stove, no refrigerator, no furniture—bare-bones. I have access to a mattress, two chairs, and a table but no fridge or stove.

"What do you think?" I ask.

"Pretty basic, kind of creepy with the morgue across the alley," she replies. "But the price is right!"

Truthfully, it is dreary, but it is cheap and in the central part of town.

"OK, let's rent it." Being the one who is employed, I am the primary renter.

Neither of us likes the morgue in the back; however, I can park in front of the main drag.

We cook soup in an electric coffeepot (I had one) and leave milk and cheese out on the windowsill to keep cold. I keep my burger-flipping job until I find something else in town. There isn't anyone else to take care of me; I have to do it myself. I can get a small refrigerator and a hot plate with my next paycheck.

Annette doesn't stay long. She decides she wants an adventure. She hooks up with a boy who is planning to hitchhike across the country. They both ask if I want to go along, but the answer is "no." I don't have time for adventures; I want to get established and figure out how to go to community college. I am on a mission.

Section 7:
Reflections

28
Back to the Beginning

Sitting on the floor, my back against the wall, I continue to search through the journals and papers from a box labeled "Past" strewn at my feet. I have no idea what the outcome of writing down my memories will be. I have set out on a path of discovery, without knowing what the journey will bring. I am aware that I have resisted draining the Well of Sorrow for many years. Now, finally, the time has come.

As I begin to remember, I feel the old tug of resistance once again: *Why should I remember when I have tried so hard to forget? I don't want to feel negative emotions, old hurts, and old harms.*

Even to myself, it sounds like a child's cry. *These memories and feelings are safely buried. Let it be!*

However, resurrecting memories and releasing emotions are acts of healing. It is time to empty the Well. It has served its purpose.

As the process begins, I realize I have not accounted for the *sorrow* in the Well of Sorrow. It's ironic since that is the name I've chosen.

At the time, I was thinking of the pain, anger, guilt, shame, bewilderment, and fear I had experienced as a child that left me scarred. I had resolved many negative emotions but not all. Feelings of sorrow, loss, and grief still stagnated at the bottom of the Well. I hadn't mourned for the child who was abandoned, whose innocence was lost, for the young girl who was assaulted, or the teenager who could not connect with her mother. Nor had I celebrated the child who was courageous and persistent, the young girl who struggled through trauma and managed to survive, the adolescent who dreamed of emancipation and achieved it.

I also hadn't resolved the feelings I had about my parents. I still held onto judgments of them, even while learning that the journey was not about judging. It was about letting go of judgments, expanding understanding, and with that, a change in perception.

Slowly, glimpses of the possibilities came as I wrote down the first memories. These I had shared with colleagues, who pointed out that I was writing at the "thirty-foot" level, looking down on experiences but not immersing myself in the emotions that went along with them.

Immersion is necessary to release the residue of memories stored in the Well. The loss of my mother and the loss of Dolly have created feelings I can acknowledge now but that I could not manage as a bewildered child. They had slipped to the bottom of the Well.

It is harder to breathe as I start to remember the mean boy and Grimes, the physical beatings, and the terror of Margaret's death. I don't want to feel those feelings again. But I haven't acknowledged the feelings of helplessness when physically subdued and violated. Immediate relief comes from recognizing and accepting the feelings. The actual act of writing is a release, an unintended consequence. I feel almost giddy with the possibilities. There are more memories where that one came from.

Embracing the idea of forgiveness or compassion for the "villains" of the story is more of a struggle. The hurt child wants to say, "*No! Why should I forgive? They hurt me!*"

Is this really about forgiveness or just letting go?

The adult in me understands forgiveness. I know forgiveness is for the benefit of the forgiver, but what about accountability? I rail against the idea that some individuals in my story are not accountable for their actions. Why should they not be responsible? Why should I have compassion for behaviors I find unfathomable? Why should I overlook the antagonists in my life when what they did was harmful? Who else has the right to judge the one who experienced the consequences of others' choices? And if individuals are not held accountable, they will harm others. That's how it works.

I need to "ken" the question of whether there is a benefit to judgment and to understanding. If not, I need to set aside the judgments I hold, to find a resolution, and to let go. I'm not sure it is possible.

Isn't there an old saying, "Let sleeping dogs lie"? Is it worth the pain to reexperience the emotions that go with these memories—emotions safely tucked away in the Well of Sorrow? I will have to bring these emotions up with the memories if I wish to be free of these experiences—the good and the bad.

I set aside my notes, get up off the floor, and move to my computer. It is time to stop thinking and start writing the memories down. *I'm going to do the memory thing, bring all this stuff up, and let it go.* The decision made, I sigh in relief and pull up papers from the box to type up notes on memories and information I already have. First, the memories, then I can do family research.

My childhood glimpses of my parents' backgrounds are enough to fuel my curiosity. But I lack information on the context that may help me to see them in a different light. Perhaps new information will change my understanding and my perception of who they are and why they made the choices they made. As the journey "to ken" commences, I know it will be essential to put in context the memories in the Well of Sorrow. I am curious: Will this context bring new understanding to me in terms of Calvin's life, Geraldine's life, my life—our lives? Will it make a difference, change my perceptions, and provide me with greater awareness? I want to know . . . to ken on a deep, emotional level.

The excavation of memories, searching for answers from the Well of Sorrow, comes first. My intention is to unearth and release the memories and feelings, and in doing so, gain understanding and peace. Almost simultaneously, I begin to explore the possibility that there are aspects of my parents' experiences that may help me understand what happened and who they were. Can I learn things that would help me let go of negative feelings toward them? Will the merging of memory and new knowledge about the context of their lives bring a better understanding of who my mother and father were? Is it a question of forgiveness or simple acceptance that it all happened, with permission to let go and move on?

I'm not sure, but I'm about to find out.

29

Reflections on Calvin, My Father

The memories I have of my father are full of fear and apprehension. There are no funny father-daughter moments of laughter, of sharing, no remembered conversations. That is not the kind of relationship I had with Calvin.

The first benefit of attending his funeral was a visceral understanding that I didn't have to be afraid anymore. Even though I hadn't seen him since I was an adolescent, a potent residue of fear and anxiety still lodged in my marrow and bone. But he was dead. There was no longer a need to hold anxiety and vigilance. There was nothing to be afraid of.

I had looked down on him in his coffin, knowing he was gone. I had been apprehensive about seeing him, alive or dead. There was a surprising release of fear and anxiety as I accepted it was over. Unexpectedly, I felt a moment of sadness for losing a father I had never known and would know only from information gathered from other sources. I was left with piecing together the story of his life.

Taking time to get acquainted with my father's background helps me to think of him in a different light with a different perspective. The combination of knowledge and memories fuses to a better understanding of the circumstances . . . perhaps not enough for forgiveness, but at least empathy for who he was and how he might have come to be who he was.

Thinking about his funeral, I remember the photograph and card Becky had found in his bedroom. Why did he carry the picture of me as a young child with him through multiple moves for more than forty years? Who was I in his eyes? It was a mystery that tugged at my heart. *Is there more here than I know?* What was the import of his final legacy?

I search for something that will help me understand what happened. What do I know? Will this new information generate a different perspective?

It does.

I knew little about my father's family except a vague memory of visiting a great-uncle's farm in Texas.

My closest family contact is Aunt Daisy. She is the holder of family information that I will need to begin a more thorough search. I call her first.

"Hi, Aunt Daisy. Diana here. How are you?"

"Getting on well enough. How about you?"

"I'm good. I called because I'm working on writing about my childhood and would like to learn more about Calvin's family. Can you help me?"

"Of course," she says in that soft voice I remember so well. "I'll get some things together for you."

"Great! I'm coming down to California in a few weeks. I'll come to visit, if that's OK."

Driving out to Daisy's, I think about all the times she has helped in those early years in California.

She was a safe haven in a chaotic world when Margaret was our stepmother.

I pull into the trailer park and drive to the end where Jack and Daisy's mobile home is parked. Jack sits in his usual place basking in the sun, on the side yard.

"Hi, Jack. Looks like you are enjoying the sun." He appears more stooped and frail than the last time I saw him, but he is getting on in years, so that is not unexpected.

"Yes. Daisy is inside waiting for you."

I walk up the steps to the front door, stopping to call out to Daisy before I enter. "Hello, Daisy. It's me, Diana. Can I come in?"

Opening the screen door, I enter the trailer and join Daisy in the kitchenette. She looks the same as she always has—tall and thin, dressed in a cotton dress with the ever-present apron around her middle. Her dark hair frames a face more creased and wrinkled but with the familiar smile. She has a cup of coffee waiting for me on the counter.

"Hello, Diana. It's good to see you. Do you want sugar in your coffee? Or milk?"

"No, thanks. How are you?"

"Good enough. Jack has rheumatism pretty bad, and he forgets things. He doesn't get around much. What are you up to?"

"No good," I laugh. "Actually, as I mentioned on the phone, I am doing some family research. I'd like to learn more about Calvin's family."

"Yes, of course. I put together the information I have. It's in this manila envelope. These are copies, so you can have everything in there."

"Thanks, Daisy! I appreciate it." I open the package and pull out several photocopied pages of information.

"See here," Daisy says, pointing. "This is a list of family members across the generations and their birth dates. My mother copied it from the family Bible."

"This looks very helpful. I'll start searching and let you know what I learn from my search."

"Diana, while we are talking about family, there is something I want to tell you," Daisy begins. "I know you have hard feelings about your grandmother Maude, but you should know she tried to leave Grimes several times. She had no skills, and in the end, went back to him even though he was abusive. It was hard for women in her time to leave their husbands, even if they were abusive."

"Thanks. I'll keep that in mind as I sort through the family history."

There are exciting tidbits in the envelope that she gave me. I smile when I realize that the men in the family were often named after US presidents in office at their birth, and then sons were named after their fathers. I see the spread of family across states and time. Just this little bit of information is revealing.

But this process requires time. The details Daisy provided will be useful when I begin the family search in earnest. The manila envelope remains in the box marked "Past" until I finally decide it is time to learn more.

It is several years after my retirement before I can turn my attention to a full-on search for family history. I locate the manila envelope Daisy had given me as I unpack the "Past" box. I am already immersed in writing down my memories, so I call my nephew Haydn, my brother John's grandson.

"Haydn, I was wondering if you might be interested in a summer job? I'm busy writing my memoir and want to know if you have some time to help me. I need some help doing research on the family tree, particularly Calvin's. Are you interested?"

"Yes, I love doing this kind of research!"

"Great! What I want you to do is an online search for family information, including genealogy and context for the places family members lived."

"Sure!" he says.

"Haydn, you're supposed to ask how much I'm paying."

"OK, how much are you paying? And I can't work past September when school starts."

"I'll pay you up to three hundred dollars, at fifteen dollars an hour to see what you can find out. We can revisit after that, depending on how much information you have been able to locate."

"OK, sounds good."

Haydn does an excellent job. We piece together a comprehensive picture of my father's family. Searching through national archives, the census, and search engines, both free and commercially available, we are able to map a family history that spans 350 years.

I have a family with roots! And they are long roots to 1690 and earlier—roots in the early colonization of Virginia, roots in a family with a long heritage in America before it was America.

My father's family were among the passengers of the first five French Huguenot ships that brought refugees to America, fleeing religious persecution in France. The story of the Ammonette family was the story of an American family, rooted in a search for religious freedom. Like many American families, sons were born, spread west to seek their own land and place in an expanding America. My family sent sons to fight in every American war, including the American Revolution and every conflict since the colonies formed a Union, including Vietnam, Iraq, and Afghanistan.

What we learn provides an unexpected sense of rootedness that I had not had before. I have been moved around, unanchored, throughout my childhood. This family history helps me feel grounded. I have a family that was part of the American fabric. I have always identified myself as American, but now I feel *more* like an American. It's funny how unexpectedly roots can mean a lot. I can identify with my father. Having a family for the first time, I understand why he had insisted that we, his children, were American.

By the time the genealogy search reached my father's generation, the affluent parts of the ancestry had morphed into scrubland farmers living in Oklahoma Indian territory.

Maude, my paternal grandmother, was born in 1896 in Territory 4, Chickasaw Country, in what would become part of Oklahoma State. She attended school until third grade. At some point, the family moved from the territory to a small town in southwestern Oklahoma. The data was sparse but suggested that the Ammonette family had its share of hardships in this frontier state.

When Maude was eighteen, she met and married James Harvey English, and my father was born in October 1916. James worked alongside his father as the territorial postman, delivering mail to rural towns and farms. James died a victim of the 1918 Spanish flu epidemic, leaving Maude, an uneducated, unskilled widow, with a two-year-old child near the start of the '20s.

My grandmother's betrayal of me as a child cuts deep. I don't want to take into consideration that Maude had few choices in her time. I know that it is true, but I don't want to feel sympathy for her. Now, however, I can imagine what it would be like to lose her husband, her father, and her brother in a short period.

As a young widow with a two-year-old child in rural Oklahoma, Maude had few options. She met and married Grimes, and my father's childhood was sealed. Grimes, I was told by Daisy, "viciously" abused my father physically from early childhood. This abusive home life was likely why the 1930 census showed my father employed as a barber's assistant at age thirteen. My father was on his own at an early age as Oklahoma faced the devastation of the Dust Bowl years. Maybe that was why he let each of his children go in our early-to-middle teens. He had done it himself.

The trouble with additional information is that it can change my perception. I am startled to find I can empathize with Calvin's experience of abuse. I can understand why he might have been the way he was and how he perpetuated his own experiences onto his children.

It is a surprise to find census records showing that despite his difficult childhood, my father went back to school in his late teens. He had some ambition but few skills or education. And he had a propensity to propagate rather than accumulate. Other than the times he was despondent enough to try to kill himself, he worked and supported his household . . . glimmers of a man I never knew.

I realize that my father, like all of us, was a man of his time and circumstances. He might have been loved by his mother, but he wasn't protected. His model of fatherhood was a viciously violent man. He had to find his own way without the benefit of support and guidance.

It was, I think, unusual for a man in the early 1950s to take custody of and raise four children—not that he "raised" us, but he kept us in his possession. The basics were provided in terms of food and shelter, most of the time, but not much else. He held my siblings and me together, each one peeling away as early as possible.

I am forever grateful for the sibling connections.

Calvin was responsible for that. My mother would have split us up.

Besides working, my father's approach to managing was to bring women, sometimes women he barely knew, into our household as "mothers." My father's legacy included other things than negative emotions. My siblings and I got our "clean gene" and "worker gene" from my father. He was always personally clean, and he required a clean-living environment: dishes done, floors swept, beds made, things put away. He always worked. Even in the Great Depression, he had a job on a farm. My guess was his own physical abuse contributed to his anger issues and violent discipline. He was also a product of his time and culture. It was not enough to say that he was a victim himself and that victimization excuses everything.

Being a victim is not a license to be irresponsible. Many victims of abuse manage to treat their children nonviolently.

My father had serial relationships with women. He had to have had some charm because he didn't have money. He never seemed to be without a woman in his life from early adolescence to his death. He produced children at a prolific level and took on the care of his wives' children. Each of his wives brought risks of their own that I had to navigate. I doubted my father deliberately brought a juvenile pedophile into our household when I was a child.

As I explore past memories, I think the predominant feeling I should hold is anger at being violated, assaulted, and forced to become acquainted with fear. That isn't the case. The feelings still hidden in the Well are not anger but sorrow, grief, and loss: sadness and grief for the little girl who felt helpless and was defenseless; the double-whammy loss of my mother and Dolly, my comfort in a comfortless world; and the loss of innocence and enhanced feelings of vulnerability from assaults by males in my life. Fortunately, I have my brothers to counter those experiences so that my view of males is not totally distorted.

I am overwhelmed with feelings of sadness for that little girl: sad when I remember the ragamuffin child creeping along the edges of the room, her back against the wall, treading softly so the floor wouldn't creak and alert the mean boy to her presence; sad for the child who hid at the back of the closet, behind the coats, so she wouldn't be discovered; sad that any child, let alone *this* child, would have to go through such experiences. Yet I feel pride for her grit and for working with what she had, for trying to protect herself. Sometimes she was successful; sometimes she wasn't. Part of me thinks that I was a courageous and spunky little girl.

Calvin's legacy as a father was emotional, psychological, and physical traumas. Despite this legacy of fear, I never hated my father. I was afraid of him, yes, but I didn't hate him. His household was one to be endured.

As I learn more about his background, I see glimmers of a man

I never knew and never would. I see pictures of him laughing and playing with my older siblings.

By the time I was born, that laughter had disappeared. Other forces were at play.

It is odd to come to this point in my reflection and realize that part of me has always suspected my father loved me, even if I didn't have feelings of love for him.

There was nothing overt—no words—but some actions that suggested he cared. As bad as the violence was, he mostly left me alone. He refused to let us be separated as a sibling group. He always worked to provide, even if the provision was minimal. He bought me glasses when I couldn't see and let me go to school camp. He let us go to Switzerland and England and didn't respond to my challenge when we returned. He could have abandoned us or split us apart when we returned to America, but he didn't do that.

He was abused as a child, unprotected by his mother.

This fact doesn't excuse his behavior, but it does mitigate it. It is helpful to have this context. Through this process of researching my father's past, I no longer feel inclined to judge him. The facts speak for themselves. I can understand both his personal and cultural context. He did what he did, the best he could under the circumstances. I have realized it isn't a question of forgiveness. What happened, happened, and cannot be undone.

I don't think he was a bad man; he worked hard, he did his best, and he didn't have a lot of happiness.

I also learn that through adversity comes strength. I am strong enough to survive, and I am strong enough to let the past dissipate, knowing that beyond any judgment I might make, his life and its end speak for themselves. It isn't even about forgiveness but accepting his behavior for what it was, knowing that people eventually reap what they sow.

He died alone. He didn't have his family or his children around him in his life or his death.

I don't have to judge. I find more sadness because I never knew him as a person or even as a father other than a terrifying force to be avoided whenever possible. I understand that he was trapped by his circumstances: lack of education, skills, positive parenting, and connections. And finally, it seems deeply sad that he never knew me as a daughter. I'm pretty cool, so he really missed out.

Somehow, he got a lovely place for his final rest. He liked sitting under trees, and he was laid to rest under an oak or sycamore tree with broad arms. He must have done something right.

What I learn from this process of remembering and finding new information about my father is that I can't change what happened. I can change how I think about what happened. I can change my perceptions, improve my understanding, and know and see differently to gain or find empathy.

In a word, I can ken.

30

Reflections on Geraldine, My Mother

I am back on the floor in my office for the last time, searching through the box marked, "Past." I look for pictures and mementos of my mother. My feelings about my mother loom large as I shuffle papers. Reflecting on our relationship is more complicated, more nuanced, and more difficult than I thought it would be.

I had long believed I'd come to terms with it over the years. There had been more opportunity, for good or ill, to know who she was, both in my adolescent and adult life.

Can I learn anything new by remembering and collecting more information about my mother's history and family? What am I trying to ken? Who she was? Why she left? Why she didn't love me?

While my father came from an impoverished background, was uneducated, and lacked skills, that was not true of my mother. Geraldine Lothian Paton Reid was the daughter of a wealthy Scottish family. The family wealth came from her mother's side and social status from her father's family. Gerald, my grandfather, was educated at Oxford and served as an officer in the British Army. His wife, Margaret, my grandmother, was the heir of the family publishing business founded by Robert Clark in Edinburgh. While not considered a beauty, she was an heiress. A year after Margaret and Gerald's union, my mother was born. She was an only child until she was sixteen, when Margaret became pregnant despite Gerald's absence serving with the British Army in India. The pregnancy resulted in a significant rift between mother and daughter. These experiences shaped who my mother was and who she would become.

My mother could never accept her half brother, Peter. In her words, "My father is not Peter's father. He is illegitimate."

After the pregnancy rift with her mother, Geraldine was dispatched to Oxford's Girls' School where she met my father, Calvin, an American soldier stationed at a nearby military base, on an excursion into town. By the time she was seventeen, Geraldine was pregnant with my brother John. Her rebellion ended in pregnancy and forced marriage to my father. There would be no shame brought to the Paton Reid family name. Geraldine was consigned to a life with Calvin.

The seeds of my mother's lifelong resentment of being "cheated" out of her inheritance had been sown with the birth of her brother. Not only did my mother now have a male sibling as competition, but she also was no longer the sole heir. My mother never felt she got her fair share, even though she was also the beneficiary of a trust set up by her maiden aunts. Even the trust was not enough for my mother because it was split into two: half for her, half for her brother.

Clearing out her papers after her death was a revelation for my sister and me. Our mother had tried multiple times to break the money trust left to us, her children. My mother was willing to pilfer her children's inheritance when she found she could not live "adequately" on her own inheritance funds. There was ample evidence in the paperwork that she lied to the lawyers, claiming she needed to support her children. The only child my mother supported was her son Jamie, fathered by Stanley.

Shuffling through the papers in the box, I find the last photograph I have of my mother, taken after she had relocated from Cornwall, England, to Galway, Ireland.

I was in Dublin at a work conference and took the opportunity to take the train to Galway to see my mother. I had no expectation that I would ever again return to Ireland after this visit, and she was unlikely to make a trip to the United States. I wanted to try again to connect; it was the last time I saw her before she died.

In the photo, taken by Billie, the gardener, we sat at the wrought iron table at the back of the cottage in Galway. This was the visit when Geraldine and I had "the talk," when she said she was sorry for leaving us as children. Sitting with her there on the patio, I looked first at my mother and then out over the magnificent garden she had created. The gray-blue water of Lough Corrib and the lush green of the Galway hills were a backdrop to her garden.

My mother's skin looked pasty, and lines of burst blood vessels wilted across her cheeks. Her eyes were already glazed from her morning gin. The plants, in contrast, were lush and green. The buds of the spring flowers were about to burst forth in glorious color.

How could she be such a wonderful gardener but fail to nurture and grow her own children?

This is a question I will never have the answer to.

As we sat in the sunshine looking across to the Lough, I thought it was unlikely we'd reconnect. Nothing seemed to have changed. I was expecting a polite talk about village life or an update on Jamie.

However, without preamble, avoiding eye contact, she took a sip of her gin in the morning sun and said, "I'm sorry. I'm sorry for leaving you as children. Can you forgive me?"

I couldn't explain to her that it wasn't about forgiveness but connection. I didn't think of my mother in terms of forgiveness. I had already come to terms with her choices as they related to me many years earlier. From my view, she was who she was. And while my attempts had failed, I still wanted to connect with her, though the need to connect had become less urgent as the years passed. I didn't understand her, which hadn't changed in all the years I knew her.

I opened my mouth, and the words came out in a rush. "What is done is done and cannot be undone. I would rather not have had the experiences I had, but they helped make me who I am today. I like who I am."

As I spoke, she looked away across the garden. She wanted more, but I didn't have more to give. These words were the best I could do. She took another sip of gin.

It seems serendipitous that the next photo out of the box is one of my earliest memories of my mother. Johnny, Patsy, and I are in the picture, my mother out of frame, in the background.

We were on holiday in Fowey in Cornwall, the time we spent together before she abandoned us. These were happy times of laughter and connection with my mother and my siblings. I was safe, secure, and living a life full of laughter and adventure. How did it go from happy to terrifying? Everything changed. I realized only later that during our happy holiday she was planning to abandon us.

The years between then and the next time I saw my mother were filled with violence, fear, anxiety, assault, and death. What little comfort I had in the new chaos disappeared overnight, just like my mother. Mostly I was bewildered and lost. I focused on trying to protect myself. I stuffed my feelings into the Well of Sorrow and tried to navigate my world as best I could. I stumbled through the days and months and years focused on getting through one day to the next, wanting to know but not knowing why she left and never came back. If she didn't love me, what did that say about me?

Near the bottom of the box, I find photographs from the trip to Switzerland and when David and I lived in England as adolescents. The Swiss pictures shows my siblings and me with my mother at a chalet resort in the mountains outside Lausanne.

In swimsuits, we were fishing and swimming.

There was also the memory of that fateful response from my mother when I asked why she left us with Calvin.

I can clearly see her, even now, standing at the window with her back to the room, her shoulders slumped, staring off into the distance.

"Why, why did you leave us?" I had asked.

Her back stiffened, and after a long silence, she said, "I left Calvin because he was too violent."

I couldn't form the words to say, "I am the ten-year-old child who is the recipient of the violence you could not tolerate."

I wanted to ask, "How could you walk away?" But she confirmed what I already knew in my heart: she didn't love me/us, she didn't care about what happened to us, she couldn't be trusted. Her disclosure shocked me. And then she sent us back again.

Is it worse to lose faith from a thousand cuts or from blunt force?

With my mother, it was a thousand cuts.

As a mother myself, I find it inexplicable that a mother could leave her children in those circumstances. It is beyond my ken.

My gratitude to my mother for those two years in Cornwall is at war with the sorrow of the intervening life with Calvin. She did provide us with respite, and I am grateful for that. The trouble is, her life with Stanley was not exactly stellar—alcohol, meanness, infidelity, lies, and deceit.

It was a different set of issues from those we faced in Calvin's household. There was no physical or sexual assault, but there was an emotional assault from Stanley. While those two years didn't resolve issues I had with my mother, they were lifesavers, and for that my mother must have credit. She bought us "proper" clothes and exposed us to another world through travel. She gave us a hiatus from my father's house. She had my teeth fixed, which was a massive boost to my self-esteem. More importantly, after completing my work in the hotel, I was free to roam wherever I wished.

Living in Cornwall was a lifesaving sojourn, despite the pain of failing to find the mother I had hoped for. Perhaps she didn't know how to be a mother, especially of adolescents. She knew virtually nothing about us when we went to live with her. She was immersed in the life of the pub, and probably already on the way to being an alcoholic. Her life with Stanley was unhappy. It was not the best time to try to parent two American adolescents who had been released into the paradise of Cornwall.

In its own way, learning about my mother's family does make a difference. It provides a sense of rootedness, similar to learning about my father's family. The two family histories are different, but each is gratifying in its own way. I feel a sense of pride when I realize that the R & R Clark printing company published some fantastic authors, including Rudyard Kipling and Bernard Shaw.

I was born into a family that produced books. That's cool. However, it was apparent that wealth and status did not necessarily result in happiness. It also helped me understand what a far fall my mother had from her wealthy upbringing to life with my father.

In reflection, there is some injustice in my mother's treatment when she was seventeen. I cannot think that anyone in the family approved of my mother's behavior.

Still, Margaret was successful in covering up her own out-of-wed-lock pregnancy. She undoubtedly could have helped my mother had she wanted to. It wouldn't have been the first time an unplanned pregnancy had occurred in English or Scottish "society." But Margaret had no intention of risking the family name because of her daughter's indiscretion. From Margaret's perspective, my mother had "made her bed" and could have no recourse but to lie in it, in America.

Still, I continue to struggle with my perception of my mother. It is the abandonment that got in the way—the sheer disregard of it.

She was "escaping for herself," not caring enough about her children to see to it that they were safe.

However, through this process of remembering and learning about my mother's family, there is a slight change in perception. At the very least, the process has created a space for a better understanding. Although resistant, I cannot deny I am beginning to see her in a more sympathetic light. As my understanding and knowledge increases, I find I can be more open to the possibility of Geraldine as someone other than a mother. I begin to see her as a human being with her own trials and tribulations.

She was also a daughter and a woman, as well as a mother.

This understanding doesn't erase her actions or their consequences but does add some level of perspective.

I just wanted her to love me as a child, as well as an adolescent, and I could not understand why she didn't.

I can see how a lack of support from her own mother could influence her decisions. However, she had resources, a substantial monthly allowance from the trust set up by her aunts, and other wealthy family members she could have turned to. She had a father she adored who could have supported her. She had options, although she may not have felt like she did. Perhaps she saw marriage to my father as an out. She didn't really know who he was or his background until the first time she went to Texas, although she already knew he had lied to her about being married and having a child. Instead, she ran away and left us to our fate with Calvin. Nothing I learned provided a satisfactory answer to why she did that.

Through this process of getting to ken, it becomes clear that I have not come to terms with my feelings about my mother as well as I thought I had. I find myself resistant to remembering who she was, remembering how I felt.

As I remember those times, I believe my mother made some effort to be what she thought a mother should be, and those efforts resulted in some successes. She made an effort, which is important.

I call John to talk to him about the trouble I am having reflecting on our mother. I think he might have a different perspective because he is older, the one who was with her the longest.

"John, I'm really having trouble writing about Mother. I just don't understand her at all."

He pauses for a moment and says, "She was a very private person . . . introverted."

OK, maybe. I'd like to press him for more information, but he is ill, and I am reluctant to add to his burdens.

Introversion doesn't feel like enough explanation. It doesn't explain the decisions she made. It hurt to realize she had already planned to abandon us that last summer in Fowey.

While we were catching crabs and having snail races, she was thinking about how and when to abandon us. She had already taken up with Stanley and was prepared to leave us when we returned to Cheshire from holiday.

Despite this realization, I am grateful for that holiday because it solidified my relationship with my siblings. We spent that summer together, and John and Patsy were kind to me, and I, in turn, to David.

But what was she doing? Soaking up memories of her children before she abandoned us? It leaves me breathless to think her abandonment was intentional.

Sighing, I take a deep breath, shifting my position against the wall. Taking a sip of water, I continue with my reflection.

The hardest part of my relationship with my mother was wanting her to be something that she wasn't and could not be. I wanted to love her and for her to love me. I wanted her to love me enough to take care of me, to protect me, to mother me as a child, and to be there for me as an adolescent and an adult. I wanted her to see me, to know me as a person, as her daughter. I couldn't find love for her, and I never felt that she loved me, at least not after Switzerland.

I am saddened she did not lead a happy life.

In many ways, her life was tragic. The task of being a mother, at least to us, was beyond her. It was very sad to remember that she died alone, at night, on the dirt floor of an Irish cottage.

I find this a sorrow in its own right—an end no one would want.

Sometimes I think of her as a broken bird. The imagery comes to mind mostly because her left hand was deformed due to injuries from a car accident. Her left thumb was bent, broken in the crash, hanging at an odd angle. I don't know why she didn't get it fixed, perhaps as a reminder of the miscarriage that occurred due to the accident. I don't know the whole story.

She told me that she blamed Stanley for the accident, miscarriage, and injuries.

As I think back on it, there was always something broken about my mother. I do not think she had a happy life, although it was adventurous.

She was wounded by Stanley's unfaithfulness, but they were both unfaithful to each other, having affairs over the years but still staying together. Later, when Stanley was dying, she saw to it that he was cared for until the end, and his brother did the same for her to her end. Whatever connection there was, it was strong because they stayed together, even as they repeatedly betrayed each other. She did not lead a charmed life. In retrospect, her life was not charmed at all. I hadn't realized that before.

I can't judge my mother because I can't comprehend her choices.

Except for the time she locked me up in the tower so I wouldn't make "the same mistakes" she did, she didn't exhibit what I would call maternal behaviors. Her words told me she thought that we, her children, were "mistakes." Was that actually my mother being honest? She viewed me as a mistake?

I conclude that it is not just us who lost out on a mother. My mother lost out on having children.

Her Well of Sorrow must have been profound indeed.

31

Final Reflections—Serendipity and Random Acts of Kindness

I am lucky.

I was nurtured as a young child, which helped me to survive the ensuing chaos in my life. My mother was responsible for that. I didn't know what changed, but by 1953 she was ready to bolt. She did what some women did then and now . . . found a man to run away with—without her children.

But I do have my mother to thank for a stable, safe, and secure early childhood. Though she hired a nanny to take care of the day-to-day details, she bears credit for producing a happy, gregarious child. My earliest childhood memories are full of adventure and laughter.

I was excited about exploring the world, unafraid of what might be around the next corner. I was connected, part of a family, which was why the change was so shocking. The relationships with my siblings were essential . . . the glue that held me together. I knew what loving and connected felt like.

While I can mourn the loss of security and care, I can also aspire to regain a semblance of those feelings.

For the longest time after my mother left, I was bewildered and confused. I couldn't make sense of my surroundings. I didn't understand where she was or why our life had changed. She had been my refuge and comfort.

Then I didn't have a lot of time to grieve my mother or Dolly when

I lost her too. Life narrowed to a focus on getting through each day. Serendipity.

I was free from assault for a while after that, then circumstances changed again. We moved to California, to my grandmother's house. There I perfected the art of dissociation, separating myself from what was happening to me as I fell into the clutches of Grimes. I felt insignificant, overwhelmed by feelings of helplessness as he towered over me in the shadow of the night light. It was easier for me to slip away to a distant place where I could not see and feel what was happening.

Finally, I found the courage to speak up. My pious, churchgoing grandmother supported her husband, the pedophile.

Fortunately, there was some respite before the next trauma. May was there for a while, and life was stable, if not nurturing. And, when May left yet again, Patsy stepped in as a child mother. Life was as everyday as it could be in these circumstances. My sister balanced my father's erratic behavior, including his attempt to commit suicide and failure to buy food.

In my middle childhood, Aunt Daisy provided a bird's-eye view of what "normal" life might look like. She was a guardian angel for a while in the most traumatic years and was a source of support and normalcy. We played games like Clue and Monopoly, watched television, ran under the sprinkler in the front yard, did things that normal kids do. It was a relief, and Daisy's was a place where I didn't have to feel hypervigilant all the time. We had sleepovers and explored the woods and fields around our neighborhood. These glimpses of normalcy were a balm to a fractured child trying to hold on—and provided hope.

Daisy was always supportive and kind. She gave me hope until we moved away from where she lived, and my second stepmother, Margaret, arrived. About this time, my sister, at age fifteen, left to get married. I was shell-shocked before Margaret and her children arrived, and their presence only intensified the dire circumstances.

Beatings were not the worst that happened. Hands down, Margaret's drowning was the worst of the traumas thus far. I knew about death; I'd seen it before. But the drowning was literally in my face. And I thought I was going to die too. I was terrified of potential repercussions and full of guilt and shame for my death wish.

The years in England saved my life. Although I failed to establish a meaningful connection with my mother, I discovered a meaningful relationship with myself, learned I could provide for myself and survive, and gained enough confidence in myself that I could stand up to my father upon our return to America.

I would be remiss in these reflections if I did not emphasize other essential influences that impacted my childhood: my bloodline, siblings/connections, the role of serendipity, and the importance of random acts of kindness.

All of these helped to pave a path forward to survival.

First, though, I claim genetics as a contributor to survival as well—a solid, sturdy constitution consisting of a combination of genes from immigrants, pioneers, and entrepreneurs . . . plus a healthy dose of French and good sturdy Scottish stock added to the mix, which I'm sure explains something about who I am. While my father influenced my daily life, I think my Scottish genes influenced who I was and who I am, even from the earliest days.

I had a forthright nature: someone who said things on her mind, sometimes without censor. This trait caused trouble for me as a child as well as an adult.

Other characteristics can include bravery, ingenuity, and stubbornness, especially the latter. Perhaps "determination" is a better word. A love of nature and raw beauty sustained me then and now, a regenerative factor essential to my well-being. I have a solid constitution.

I am reminded of this by a picture of my mother I find in the "Past" box. I see I inherited her physique. Like my mother, I was a bonny lass, and canny.

I learned early that it was better to avoid being knocked down if I could help it, so I developed skills in assessing and avoiding risk.

The presence of "guardian angels" was another saving grace.

I am grateful for Patsy.

She was a lifesaver at a critical time and an anchor for me throughout my life. She provided the bridge to survival until I could manage to protect myself, and later, David.

My fervent wish is that all younger siblings could have the kind of support my sister provided, even though she was a child herself. Her presence throughout my life has been essential. While my sister has a starring role in my life, that is not to underestimate my brothers, John and David and later Jamie. They are vital to me in different ways and fundamentally good people.

Johnny was my hero and someone I looked up to. David, my little brother, was someone I needed to protect. Most of my experiences with males were negative and abusive, so it was critical to have a counterbalance in my life.

In terms of serendipity, random acts have ripple effects, sometimes to one's benefit.

My years from ages five to eleven were traumatic years, but serendipity also played a role. My early childhood experiences served as a buffer in the bad times, as did my siblings. But I was assaulted by the mean boy and Grimes, betrayed by Maude, and witnessed Margaret's death. The mean boy was removed from my proximity because something happened to someone else. Serendipity and a little courage on my part were responsible for the end of the abuse by Grimes. Margaret's death was devastating, but I believe serendipity was at play. Logic suggested I should have drowned that day. Her superior strength, terror, and my poor swimming skills all point to the likelihood that I should have drowned as she did.

Reflection and a little research suggest that at the end of her struggle, Margaret may have experienced hypothermia, a condition that can cause a loss of muscle strength based on the length of time she was in the water. Swimming in icy snowmelt, in bottomless pools, is a known contributor to drowning in this particular river. My guess is that Margaret's strength diminished during the minutes I tried to save her. This reflection—a little balm—helps relieve some of the guilt I felt for wishing her dead.

Random acts contributed to my survival more than planned activity, for which I am grateful.

Moving to England and living in a hotel was a rather unusual experience. I had to navigate a new household and a new set of relationships, but the place superseded the living arrangements. For the first time, I understood how important a place can be in terms of a personal sense of well-being. I felt whole and complete, living by the water, feeling the wind on my face every day. The wildness of the coast resonated internally and externally. The sheer joy of living by the water influenced choices about where I would live for the remainder of my life.

As I look back at the totality of my childhood . . . yes, I experienced terrible, traumatic things that I had to cope with, in real time and afterward, along with focusing on basic survival. But I did it. I survived, managed with my siblings' help, a stable early childhood, and sometimes serendipity and random acts of kindness.

However, this situation is not exclusive to me. It happens to millions of children every year.

Simple *random acts of kindness* were also key to my ability to survive and thrive across childhood. The kindness of others gave me faith and hope and helped me traverse life circumstances. While the trip to Switzerland was traumatic, it also gave me a window into a new world, and if I could find a way out of my circumstances—if I could endure—I would get there.

In addition to Patsy and Daisy, there were others along the way who were kind people outside my home environment. They may not even have understood the impact of their kindness, but these acts were important to me: Mrs. Penwith, who taught me accounting, as well as the grandmother in Plymouth who lectured the Tellam girls and me about our poor planning skills—I never forgot her words or her kindness in taking us in and feeding us, but she also imparted the wisdom, "If you find yourself in trouble, you haven't planned well enough in advance"—sage words to live by. That was when I started to learn planning as an approach to life. Then there was the school secretary in Vacaville who offered me a job on the weekend; this enabled me to get out of the house and earn money. I'm also grateful to the school counselor who helped me get school credit for my work in England to complete early high school graduation.

These experiences gave me glimpses into another world of kind and caring people and reinforced my understanding that there was a counterbalance to the world I lived in. Knowing there was a different world—a world that had kind people in it—helped me and gave me hope and the ability to cope and survive.

I would not underestimate the importance of true friendship. Having Lydia as my friend in Cornwall was enormously important to me—I felt normal, like other kids. I had a friend—someone to talk to, laugh with, have adventures with, and work through the transition of a girl moving into young womanhood. Friendship, coupled with the freedom of Cornwall, was precisely what I needed to grow and thrive into adolescence.

I always think of Lydia as my first friend, and I am sad we did not remain connected after I left Cornwall.

I wanted my parents to be something they were not and could not be. They were who they were: my mother and father with all their issues. I thought when I began this process that my father was the villain. Yet, I found more empathy for my abusive father than I did for my elusive mother. That was a surprise.

I worry for other children growing up in circumstances similar to mine. How are they surviving? And I wonder how children cope if they do not have siblings or are not able to stay connected with their siblings. Sibling connections are such a fundamental aspect of survival that I hope for all who have siblings to value those relationships. If sibling relationships have gone askew, it is important to reestablish those linkages. Connections are important.

Finally, this journey to ken has been exciting and challenging, and sometimes grueling. It was hard work to remember things I didn't want to remember and feel what I didn't want to feel again. Learning things from my research that caused a shift in tightly held perceptions of my mother and father is a surprise and benefit.

I encourage all readers to find your path to ken and understand what happened to you. Don't do as I did and bury your feelings in a Well of Sorrow.

About the Author

Dr. **Diana English** completed a Bachelor's, Master's, and Ph.D. in Child Welfare. She worked in both local and national public and private agencies with a focus on protecting children and strengthening families. With over 90 publications on child abuse and neglect, Dr. English is considered a national expert on child maltreatment; Dr. English is currently retired and lives in Seattle, Washington.